Table of Contents

I0142776

Welcome to Your Writing Adventure

Imagine a guide who has read more stories than any person alive—every myth whispered around ancient fires, every word etched into clay tablets and stone, every page of parchment inked by medieval scribes, and every thrilling bestseller that's topped modern charts. This guide doesn't just read; it absorbs, analyzes, and uncovers the hidden patterns that make stories unforgettable. It understands the epic rise and fall of heroes, the nuanced dance of relationships, and the delicate threads that weave suspense, laughter, and heartbreak into tales that linger in our hearts.

Meet AI: the most voracious reader in history, the ultimate pattern recognizer, and now, your personal writing coach. But here's the secret—no matter how much AI has read, no matter how many patterns it has uncovered, there is one thing it cannot replicate: your creativity. Your unique voice, your lived experiences, your imagination—that's where the true magic lies. This isn't a replacement for your creativity; it's a partnership designed to amplify it.

Think of AI as a collaborator that brings its boundless library of insights to your table, helping to refine your vision, guide your structure, and inspire new ideas. The spark of creation will always come from you, and the tools within this book will help you transform that spark into something the world is eagerly awaiting. Together, we'll explore the timeless art of storytelling and use the power of AI to unlock doors to creative possibilities you never thought possible.

Whether you're picking up the pen for the first time, wrestling with half-finished drafts, or searching for fresh inspiration to push your craft to the next level, A.I Teaches You How to Write a Novel will meet you where you are. It's designed to guide you step by step—from nurturing your first flicker of an idea to crafting characters and plots that captivate, and finally, to refining your work into a masterpiece.

Storytelling is as old as humanity itself, yet it evolves with every generation. This is your chance to create something new, something only you can bring into the world. With AI as your collaborator and this book as your guide, you're stepping into a new era of creative partnership, where your imagination takes center stage, powered by the collective wisdom of millennia.
The stories you've been waiting to tell are waiting for you, too. Let's begin this adventure together and shape the next chapter of storytelling history.

How AI Can Transform Your Writing Journey

AI is not just a tool; it's an opportunity. By analyzing thousands of years of human storytelling—from ancient hieroglyphics to modern blockbusters—AI has identified patterns, strategies, and techniques that resonate universally. Here's how it can transform your writing journey:

- Break Through Creative Blocks: AI can generate prompts, suggest twists, and offer fresh perspectives when you feel stuck.
- Refine Your Ideas: AI helps expand and evaluate ideas, revealing possibilities you may not have considered.
- Sharpen Your Craft: From pacing to character arcs, AI tools can analyze your manuscript and provide actionable feedback.
- Save Time Without Losing Quality: Writing and revising a novel is a monumental task, but AI can streamline the process, letting you focus on your creative vision.
- Inspire Innovation: By highlighting trends in storytelling and audience preferences, AI can help you craft stories that feel both original and timeless.

Whether you're a beginner or a seasoned writer, AI offers tailored guidance to suit your needs, making the creative process more accessible and rewarding than ever before.

Why Stories Matter: Timeless Lessons in Storytelling

Stories are the threads that weave humanity together. They are how we make sense of the world, connect with one another, and leave our mark on history. From the ancient scrolls and rock carvings that told the tales of our ancestors, to the epic poems that defined civilizations, and the novels that shaped entire generations—stories have always been at the heart of human existence. They are not just entertainment; they are how we dream, inspire, and change the world.

A Legacy Written in Stone and Ink

The first stories were carved into stone and painted on cave walls— visual narratives that captured the hunt, the triumph, and the mysteries of the natural world. These early storytellers didn't just record events; they immortalized the spirit of their communities. Thousands of years later, scrolls and manuscripts carried wisdom, myths, and culture across borders and through time. The Bible, the Epic of Gilgamesh, and ancient Hindu scriptures like the Mahabharata are more than just texts—they are the foundations of civilizations, offering guidance, meaning, and identity.

Each story was a leap into the unknown. Those who told them shaped our understanding of morality, heroism, and humanity itself. These timeless narratives remind us that storytelling is an intrinsic part of who we are.

Imagination's Power to Shape Reality

Every technological marvel we celebrate today—from flying machines to artificial intelligence—once began as an idea in someone's mind, often sparked by the stories they read or imagined. Jules Verne envisioned submarines and space travel long before science made them possible. Mary Shelley gave us the concept of reanimating life with her groundbreaking novel Frankenstein. Star Trek inspired the creation of cell phones and tablets. Science fiction has driven scientific innovation, turning "what if?" into "what's next?"

Your stories hold the same potential. Inside your imagination may lie the next transformative idea—a tale that sparks curiosity, challenges norms, or inspires someone to see the world differently. Every story you write has the power to change not only minds but the course of history itself.

Stories as Universal Bridges

Stories transcend time, language, and culture. A tale told thousands of years ago can resonate with a reader today because it taps into universal truths—love, fear, ambition, hope. Whether it's Homer's Odyssey, Shakespeare's tragedies, or contemporary bestsellers like The Hunger Games, stories remind us that we are not alone in our struggles or our dreams. They connect us to a shared human experience.

Think of the impact your story could have. It could be the beacon someone needs, the escape they crave, or the spark that ignites their own creativity. Stories are bridges between individuals, generations, and worlds—your voice can add to that timeless connection.

From the Mind to the World

The journey of every story begins in the mind of a storyteller. It starts as an unshaped idea—a flicker of inspiration—and grows into something that can captivate, challenge, and inspire. Today, we live in an era where your stories can reach the world faster than ever. Technology allows us to connect with audiences across the globe, giving every writer an opportunity to leave their mark.

What begins as a seed of imagination in your mind could one day become a story that resonates with millions. A reader across the world might fall in love with your characters, be inspired by your vision, or find solace in your words. Stories are a gift we give to the future—yours could shape how generations yet to come understand their world.

The Call to Create

You, as a writer, have the potential to shape reality. The ideas in your head—the characters, the worlds, the conflicts—could one day influence technology, spark revolutions, or simply provide comfort to someone in need. The power of storytelling has no limits.

So, take the leap. Let the stories in your mind escape into the world. They might be the spark that someone else needs to dream, invent, or believe. Every story matters, and yours could be the one that changes everything.

Who Is This Book For?

Whether you're a hopeful writer dreaming of your first novel or an experienced author seeking fresh insights, this book was crafted with you in mind. Storytelling is a journey that evolves as we grow, and no matter where you are on that path, this book has something to offer—tools, techniques, and perspectives that will inspire, challenge, and guide you.

For Novices

Starting something new is thrilling, but it can also feel overwhelming. Writing a novel may seem like an insurmountable challenge, but this book is here to make the process approachable and enjoyable.

We'll break down storytelling into manageable steps, helping you shape your ideas, create unforgettable characters, and structure your plot with confidence. Along the way, you'll find practical exercises, real-world examples, and AI-powered prompts to keep you moving forward. By the end, you'll not only have a clear roadmap to follow but also the tools to transform your vision into a finished novel you'll be proud of.

This isn't just a guide—it's a supportive companion for your first leap into the world of writing.

For Seasoned Writers
As an experienced writer, you already know that the art of storytelling is as much about refinement as it is about creativity. You've faced the blank page, wrestled with tricky plotlines, and celebrated the victories of completed works. But you also understand that great writing isn't about reaching a finish line; it's about continual growth.

This book isn't here to teach you what you already know—it's here to expand on that foundation. Think of it as a whetstone for your craft, sharpening the skills you've spent years honing and keeping your storytelling instincts razor-sharp. By revisiting familiar principles, you'll not only reinforce the techniques that have worked for you in the past but also uncover new angles and approaches to elevate your writing further.

Reading books on the craft isn't just an act of learning; it's an act of mastery. It reminds you why proven methods resonate, solidifies your understanding of storytelling's timeless structures, and pushes you to refine and innovate. This book is your chance to revisit the fundamentals while exploring new, AI-powered insights that challenge you to think in fresh ways.

You'll find advanced techniques for structuring complex narratives, deepening emotional arcs, and crafting characters with layers of depth. With the unique capabilities of AI, this book offers a lens into modern storytelling trends and tools that can help you refine your writing for today's readers.

A Shared Purpose
Whether you're a novice writer looking for a way to start or a seasoned author determined to stay at the top of your game, one thing unites us all: the love of storytelling. This book is more than a guide—it's a tool to help you create stories that resonate, entertain, and endure.

For the beginner, this is your first step on an incredible journey. For the experienced writer, this is your reminder that even the sharpest minds can benefit from reflection and refinement. Writing is a craft that constantly evolves, and this book will help you evolve with it.

The stories you're meant to tell—whether they're your first or your fiftieth—are waiting. Let's shape them together.

An Invitation to Adventure

Every great novel begins with a leap of faith: the courage to explore the depths of your imagination and translate what you find into words. AI may have read more books than any of us, but it's your voice, your ideas, and your unique perspective that will bring a story to life. This book is here to guide you through the creative process, one chapter at a time.

So, are you ready to embark on this journey? Together, let's turn your spark of an idea into something extraordinary. Your adventure as a writer begins now.

Chapter 1: The Spark of an Idea

Every novel begins with a spark—a fleeting thought, a mental image, or a question that refuses to let go. For some, it's a single line of dialogue that echoes in their mind. For others, it's a vivid setting, a mysterious character, or a "What if?" question that begs to be answered. Whatever form it takes, this spark is your gateway to an entire world waiting to be built.

But where do these sparks come from, and how do you turn them into something substantial? In this chapter, we'll explore how to find inspiration, expand it into workable ideas, and evaluate which concepts have the potential to grow into a full-fledged novel.

Where Do Ideas Come From?
Ideas are all around us, waiting to be noticed. They can come from the most unexpected places: a fleeting memory, a snippet of overheard conversation, a line in a book, or even a random object on your desk. The key is to stay curious and open to possibility.

Here are some common sources of inspiration:
- Personal Experience: Life is full of raw material. Draw from your own triumphs, struggles, fears, and dreams. Even mundane moments can spark extraordinary stories when you ask the right questions.
- Observation: Pay attention to the world around you. A stranger's behavior, the way light falls on a building, or the peculiar dynamics of a crowded room can all trigger ideas.
- History and Myth: The past is filled with stories of triumph and tragedy, and myths often capture universal truths. Retelling or reimagining these tales in new ways can lead to fresh, compelling narratives.
- Current Events: The world is constantly changing. A headline, a scientific breakthrough, or a societal trend could inspire a timely and thought-provoking story.
- Dreams and Daydreams: Your subconscious is a treasure trove of creativity. Keep a notebook by your bed to jot down dreams or let your mind wander during quiet moments.

Example: J.K. Rowling reportedly imagined the character of Harry Potter on a delayed train ride. George R.R. Martin's Game of Thrones began with a simple image of direwolves in the snow. These ideas didn't arrive fully formed—they started as sparks and grew over time.

Exploring with "What If?"
One of the most powerful tools in a writer's arsenal is the question, "What if?" This question allows you to take a small idea and expand it into endless possibilities. It invites curiosity, creativity, and the freedom to imagine.

Building Ideas with "What If?"
Start with a simple scenario and explore the possibilities:
- What if an ordinary object had extraordinary powers? (e.g., J.R.R. Tolkien's One Ring in The Lord of the Rings.)
- What if a seemingly perfect world had a hidden flaw? (e.g., Lois Lowry's The Giver.)
- What if a historical event had ended differently? (e.g., Philip K. Dick's The Man in the High Castle.)

Exercise: Expand Your Spark
- Write down a single word, phrase, or image that intrigues you (e.g., "a lighthouse in a storm" or "a mysterious message in a bottle").
- Ask yourself five "What if?" questions about it. For example:
  ○ What if the lighthouse only appears during storms?
  ○ What if it's guarding something no one should ever find?
  ○ What if the protagonist receives a message from their future self in the bottle?
  ○ What if the message contradicts everything they believe?
  ○ What if others are willing to kill for the secrets it holds?

Each question deepens the idea, revealing its potential to grow into a layered story.

Separating Good Ideas from Great Ones
Not every spark will ignite a novel. Some ideas are better suited for short stories, while others may lack the depth needed for longer narratives. To evaluate your ideas, consider these tests:

1. The Depth Test
Ask yourself: Can this idea support multiple layers of story? Great novels often explore universal themes—love, loss, redemption, ambition—while also delivering engaging characters and conflicts. A great idea will feel rich with possibility, offering you a wealth of directions to explore.

2. The Curiosity Test
Ask yourself: Does this idea make you curious? A strong idea will spark questions that demand answers. If the idea excites you, surprises you, or keeps you wondering, it's worth pursuing.

3. The Emotional Test
Ask yourself: Does this idea evoke emotion?
If your idea stirs strong feelings—excitement, fear, wonder, joy—it's likely to resonate with readers as well. Writing a novel requires dedication, and an idea you're passionate about will sustain your enthusiasm throughout the process.

4. The Uniqueness Test
Ask yourself: Is this idea different or fresh enough to stand out?
While originality isn't everything (many successful stories are retellings of familiar archetypes), a unique twist or perspective can make your story memorable.

Example: Suzanne Collins combined ancient mythology with modern reality TV to create The Hunger Games. Her idea stood out because it layered familiar themes with a unique and thought-provoking setting.

Bringing It All Together
The spark of an idea is just the beginning. By staying curious, asking "What if?", and testing your concepts, you can transform a fleeting thought into a foundation for an incredible story. Remember: the stories that resonate most are the ones you're deeply passionate about. Trust your instincts, explore your creativity, and let your imagination take the lead.

Your next great idea could be one thought away. Let it spark.

Chapter 2: Finding Your Story's Natural Form

One of the first decisions you'll face as a writer is determining the natural form of your story. Should it be a concise, impactful short story or an expansive, layered novel? Both forms have unique strengths and challenges, and understanding their differences can help you shape your idea into its most powerful expression.

In this chapter, we'll explore the unique strengths of short stories, how writing them can improve your craft, and how they can grow into larger works, including novels. Along the way, we'll look at famous books that began as short stories and evolved into timeless classics, offering inspiration for your own creative journey.

The Unique Strengths of Short Stories
Short stories are like distilled bursts of creativity. They're compact, precise, and often carry a sharper focus than longer works. For writers, they offer a chance to experiment, hone their skills, and tell complete tales in a fraction of the time it takes to write a novel.

Why Write Short Stories?
Focus on Moments and Emotions:
- Short stories excel at capturing a single moment, idea, or emotional arc. They don't require sprawling backstories or intricate subplots, allowing you to zero in on what truly matters.
- Example: Shirley Jackson's The Lottery focuses on one shocking event in a small town, delivering its impact with precision and brevity.

Opportunities for Experimentation:
- Writing short stories allows you to play with structure, style, and tone without committing to the length of a novel. It's a safe space to take creative risks.

Learning Brevity and Precision:
- Short stories demand economy of language. Every word must carry weight, a skill that sharpens your overall writing.

A Fast Path to Completion:
- Unlike novels, which can take months or years, short stories can be written and revised quickly. Completing them gives you a sense of accomplishment and keeps your momentum going.

A Gateway to Publication:
- Many writers have launched their careers by publishing short stories in literary magazines or anthologies. They're an excellent way to build your portfolio and gain exposure.

Famous Books That Began as Short Stories
Some of the most celebrated novels in literary history started as short stories. These examples show how a single, focused idea can evolve into something much larger:
- Stephen King's Carrie
  - Originally envisioned as a short story about a bullied girl with telekinetic powers, King abandoned the project after a few pages. Encouraged by his wife, he expanded it into a novel, launching his career as one of the greatest horror writers of all time.
- Ray Bradbury's Fahrenheit 451
  - This dystopian classic began as a short story titled The Fireman, published in a magazine. Bradbury later expanded it into a novel, layering in deeper themes about censorship and individuality.
- Truman Capote's Breakfast at Tiffany's
  - Capote initially wrote about Holly Golightly in a short story. Realizing her character needed more room to breathe, he expanded the work into a novella that became a cultural phenomenon.
- Ken Kesey's One Flew Over the Cuckoo's Nest
  - Kesey's exploration of mental health and institutional control started as a short story written during his time at Stanford. The idea grew into a novel that defined his literary legacy.
- Alice Walker's The Color Purple
  - Walker first experimented with Celie's story in short fiction. As she explored Celie's voice and world, the story naturally grew into a novel that earned her a Pulitzer Prize.

Growing Short Stories into Novels
Short stories are often the seeds from which larger works grow. If you find yourself returning to a completed story, wondering about the characters' pasts or futures, or envisioning unexplored facets of the world, it might be time to expand it.

When Should a Short Story Become a Novel?
The Idea Demands More Space:
- A short story focuses on a moment or theme, but sometimes the idea feels unfinished. If your characters, world, or conflict beg for further exploration, it may naturally grow into a novel.

- Example: Annie Proulx's Brokeback Mountain expanded from a short story into a novella and later an acclaimed film because its emotional depth warranted further exploration.

The Characters Won't Let Go:
- If your protagonist feels bigger than the confines of a short story, it may be time to let them inhabit a novel. Complex characters often demand a longer narrative to fully evolve.

The World Calls for Expansion:
- Some settings inspire subplots and histories that can only be explored in a novel's broader scope.
- Example: J.K. Rowling's Hogwarts started as a singular idea but grew into a richly detailed world spanning seven books.

Readers Want More:
- Feedback from readers can be a strong indicator that a short story has untapped potential.

How to Expand a Short Story into a Novel
Expanding a short story into a novel requires more than just adding words. Here's how to layer complexity:

Add Subplots and Secondary Characters:
- Introduce new characters with their own arcs, adding depth and tension to the main narrative.

Explore the World in Greater Detail:
- Build on your setting's history, culture, and rules to immerse readers in your world.

Expand the Character Arc:
- Use the novel format to show how your protagonist changes over time, facing challenges and evolving.

Develop Cause-and-Effect Progression:
- Ensure each event flows logically from the last, avoiding a disjointed "and then this happened" structure.

Encouragement to Write Short Stories
Short stories are more than a stepping stone—they're a versatile form that can stand on their own or grow into larger works. They:
- Teach precision and economy of language.
- Provide a playground for experimentation.
- Offer a fast, tangible way to build confidence and momentum.
- Build a portfolio that could lead to publication or inspire future novels.

Even if you aspire to write novels, short stories are a valuable way to hone your skills and keep your creative muscles sharp.

Exercise: Discovering Your Story's Form
- Write down a single idea, word, or image (e.g., "a stormy lighthouse" or "a message in a bottle").
- Answer these questions:
  - Does this idea feel complete in a single moment? (Short story potential.)
  - Are there characters, conflicts, or subplots waiting to be explored? (Novel potential.)
  - How would expanding or condensing the story change its impact?
- Draft a brief outline for both a short story and a novel version of your idea. Compare the results to see which form feels more natural.

Conclusion
Short stories and novels are both powerful forms of storytelling. By understanding the unique strengths of short stories and their potential to grow, you can decide which form best suits your idea. Remember, every story has its natural shape—it's your job to uncover it. So, start writing that short story. Who knows? It might just be the beginning of your next great novel.

Chapter 3: The Role of Symbolism and Themes

Stories that resonate deeply with readers often share one essential quality: they speak to universal truths and experiences. Themes and symbolism are the threads that weave meaning into a story, transforming it from mere entertainment into a piece that lingers in the mind long after the last page. While the plot tells the reader what happens, themes and symbols tell them why it matters.

In this chapter, we'll explore how to identify and develop your story's theme, use symbolism to enrich your narrative, and avoid common pitfalls along the way. With actionable tips and exercises, you'll learn how to craft stories that resonate with readers on a deeper, emotional level.

What Is a Theme?
A theme is the central idea or message that runs through your story. It's the lens through which readers interpret the events and characters, offering insight into universal questions or ideas. While a theme doesn't have to be explicitly stated, it's the undercurrent that gives your work depth and meaning.

Examples of Themes in Literature
- Love and Sacrifice: Romeo and Juliet by William Shakespeare.
- The Corrupting Power of Ambition: Macbeth by William Shakespeare.
- The Fight for Freedom: The Hunger Games by Suzanne Collins.
- The Consequences of Prejudice: To Kill a Mockingbird by Harper Lee.

Universal vs. Personal Themes
Themes can be deeply personal, drawn from your own life and experiences, or they can explore universal ideas that resonate across cultures. The most powerful themes often blend the two, taking a specific experience and connecting it to something greater.

Example: Khaled Hosseini's The Kite Runner ties the deeply personal story of guilt and redemption to universal questions about forgiveness and morality.

How Themes Emerge Naturally
Not every writer begins a story with a fully formed theme in mind. Often, themes reveal themselves during the writing process as you explore your characters, conflicts, and world.

Here's how to let themes emerge naturally:
- Reflect on Emotional Beats:
  - What moments in your story stand out? Are there recurring emotions or struggles that hint at a deeper message?
- Example: In The Road by Cormac McCarthy, the recurring imagery of light and darkness reflects the theme of hope amidst despair.
- Ask What Your Story Is About Beneath the Plot:
  - Beyond the events, what questions does your story explore?
- Example: In Life of Pi, the theme of survival is intertwined with questions about faith and imagination.
- Revisit Your Draft:
  - During revisions, look for patterns, repeated imagery, or recurring conflicts. These often point to your underlying theme.

Using Symbolism to Enrich Your Story
Symbols are objects, actions, or settings that represent larger ideas. While themes provide the "big picture," symbolism offers a subtle way to reinforce your themes and add depth to your narrative.
Examples of Effective Symbolism:
- The Green Light in The Great Gatsby
  - Represents Gatsby's unattainable dream and the fragility of the American Dream.
- The Mockingjay in The Hunger Games
  - Symbolizes rebellion and hope in the face of oppression.
- The Conch Shell in Lord of the Flies
  - Reflects order and civilization, which disintegrates as the boys descend into chaos.

How to Use Symbolism Effectively
- Be Subtle:
  - Let readers discover the meaning for themselves. Heavy-handed symbolism can feel forced and detract from the story.
- Tie Symbols to Themes:
  - Symbols should support and reinforce your theme.
- Example: In Of Mice and Men, the shattered dreams of George and Lennie are symbolized through the dead mouse and the broken puppy.
- Evolve Symbols Over Time:
  - A symbol's meaning can shift throughout the story, reflecting character growth or thematic changes.
- Example: The breaking of Piggy's glasses in Lord of the Flies mirrors the loss of clarity and order.

- Use Genre-Specific Symbolism:
  - Different genres lend themselves to unique types of symbolism:
  - Fantasy: Magical artifacts as symbols of power or destiny (The One Ring in The Lord of the Rings).
  - Mystery: Ordinary objects with hidden meanings (The Maltese Falcon).
  - Romance: Tokens of love or places tied to a relationship.

Layering Themes and Sub-Themes

Most compelling stories don't rely on a single theme, they layer multiple themes to create a richer narrative. Sub-themes often complement or contrast with the primary theme, adding complexity to the story.

Example:
In The Great Gatsby, the primary theme of the American Dream's failure is layered with sub-themes of love, greed, and disillusionment. These elements work together to create a nuanced, memorable story.

Cultural Symbolism

When incorporating symbolism, it's important to consider cultural context. Symbols often carry different meanings across cultures, and understanding this context can add richness to your story—or help you avoid unintended missteps.
Example:
The phoenix, a symbol of rebirth in many cultures, represents Jean Grey's transformation in X-Men.

Tips for Using Cultural Symbols:
- Research Thoroughly: Ensure you understand a symbol's significance before using it.
- Respect the Culture: Avoid misrepresenting or appropriating symbols without context.
- Use Cultural Depth: Symbols grounded in cultural tradition can make your story feel more authentic and universal.

Common Pitfalls and How to Avoid Them
- Overexplaining Symbols and Themes:
  - Trust your readers to interpret meaning without heavy exposition.
- Clichéd Symbols:
  - Avoid overused symbols (e.g., a red rose for love) unless you add a fresh twist.

- Inconsistent Use:
  - If you introduce a symbol, follow through with its meaning consistently throughout the story.

Exercises: Deepening Your Themes and Symbols
- Discover Your Theme:
  - Write a one-sentence summary of your story. Ask, "What is this really about?" Use this to identify your central theme.
- Brainstorm Symbols:
  - List objects, places, or actions in your story that could symbolize your theme. How can you weave them into the narrative naturally?
- Layer Your Themes:
  - Identify your primary theme and brainstorm two supporting sub-themes. How can they complement or contrast with the main idea?
- Cultural Symbolism Research:
  - Choose a culturally significant symbol and explore how it could add depth to your story's theme.

Conclusion
Themes and symbolism are the tools that elevate a story, giving it resonance and depth. By exploring universal truths, connecting personal experiences to larger ideas, and using symbols thoughtfully, you can create narratives that linger in the minds of readers long after the final page.

Start small—pick one theme or symbol and experiment. As you write and revise, watch how your story's layers naturally evolve. Trust your instincts, and let your imagination guide you to deeper meaning.

Chapter 4: Writing for Your Audience

Understanding Genre Expectations
Each genre comes with a distinct set of conventions and expectations that readers bring with them when they pick up a book. These conventions serve as a framework—a familiar structure that assures readers they're in trusted territory. But they are far from rigid rules. Instead, they are opportunities for writers to craft stories that fulfill the promise of the genre while offering something fresh and unexpected. By understanding these conventions, you gain the ability to not only meet your audience's desires but also exceed them, delivering the familiar satisfaction they crave alongside the delightful surprises they didn't know they wanted.

Think of genre conventions as a bridge between you and your readers. They guide you in creating the elements your audience expects, whether it's the puzzle-solving intrigue of a mystery, the emotional highs and lows of a romance, or the immersive world-building of science fiction. At the same time, they leave room for innovation, allowing you to infuse your story with unique ideas, twists, and perspectives that set it apart.

This is where AI becomes an invaluable tool for writers. With its ability to analyze vast amounts of data, AI identifies patterns in successful books, pinpointing what resonates most with readers of specific genres. It can highlight what keeps readers engaged, reveal trends in storytelling, and even analyze audience feedback to uncover common likes and dislikes. By leveraging these insights, you can refine your story to align with reader preferences while staying true to your creative vision.

Let's explore the key expectations for major genres and how AI-driven insights can elevate your storytelling. Whether you're writing a thrilling mystery, a sweeping fantasy, or a touching romance, understanding genre conventions is crucial. Mastering these foundations will help you create stories that captivate and surprise your audience.

Genres as Promises to the Reader
Each genre comes with an unspoken agreement between you and your audience. Readers approach a mystery, romance, or science fiction book with different expectations, emotions, and desires. Here's how AI helps you make—and exceed—these promises:

1. Mystery/Thriller
The Promise: "You'll be intrigued, challenged, and rewarded with a satisfying resolution."

Mystery readers are puzzle-solvers at heart. They expect a gripping, cerebral experience, with enough clues to guess the ending—but not too soon.
- Key AI Insights:
  - Effective Twists: AI reveals that successful mysteries layer multiple twists, spaced evenly through the narrative to maintain tension. Foreshadowing is key—AI can identify subtle ways to plant clues that pay off later.
  - Reader Dissatisfaction Triggers: Reviews show that rushed endings or unresolved threads are the most common frustrations in this genre. AI can help you avoid these pitfalls by highlighting inconsistencies or missed opportunities.
- What Works and Why:
  - Gone Girl by Gillian Flynn hooks readers with an unreliable narrator, subverting their expectations with its shocking mid-point twist. AI suggests analyzing similar techniques to build suspense and surprise.
  - The Girl with the Dragon Tattoo by Stieg Larsson balances its central mystery with deeply compelling characters, a factor AI identifies as crucial for reader engagement.

2. Romance
The Promise: "You'll feel the thrill of love, the ache of obstacles, and the satisfaction of a heartwarming (or heart-wrenching) conclusion."

Romance is one of the most popular and emotionally driven genres. Readers want to connect with the characters and experience their journey as if it were their own.
- Key AI Insights:
  - Tension in the Arc: Data from successful romances shows that gradual relationship development (slow-burn) leads to higher reader engagement. AI can analyze pacing and suggest where to heighten emotional tension.
  - Fresh Takes on Tropes: Readers enjoy familiar tropes (enemies-to-lovers, forbidden love) but crave unique twists. AI tools can brainstorm innovative spins on classic ideas.

- What Works and Why:
  - Pride and Prejudice by Jane Austen showcases a slow-burn romance with misunderstandings and societal pressures, keeping readers emotionally invested. AI highlights that the key is balancing external conflicts with internal emotional growth.
  - The Kiss Quotient by Helen Hoang flips traditional roles, offering a neurodiverse protagonist that brings fresh representation to the genre.

3. Science Fiction/Fantasy

The Promise: "You'll escape to a richly imagined world and explore ideas that challenge your perspective."

Readers of these genres expect immersive settings, imaginative concepts, and characters with personal stakes amid grand plots.
- Key AI Insights:
  - World-Building Depth: AI suggests focusing on consistent rules for your world's magic, technology, or society. Successful books reveal world-building gradually, avoiding info-dumps.
  - Big Ideas: Sci-fi and fantasy readers appreciate thought-provoking themes, such as humanity's relationship with technology or the moral implications of power.
- What Works and Why:
  - Dune by Frank Herbert combines epic world-building with personal stakes, exploring ecological and political themes that resonate universally. AI recommends weaving such layers of meaning into your plot.
  - The Fifth Season by N.K. Jemisin uses multiple perspectives to build an immersive world while tackling themes of oppression and survival, proving that genre can carry heavy, thought-provoking narratives.

4. Horror

The Promise: "You'll be terrified, unsettled, and left with a lingering sense of dread."

Horror plays on primal fears, creating an emotional experience that leaves readers questioning what's lurking in the shadows.
- Key AI Insights:
  - Atmosphere over Gore: AI analysis shows that psychological horror, where atmosphere and tension build steadily, is more effective than shock-driven horror.
  - Personal Fears: The most successful horror stories tie the supernatural or external threat to personal or emotional fears (e.g., grief, guilt).

- What Works and Why:
    - The Haunting of Hill House by Shirley Jackson excels in creating unease through subtle, creeping dread rather than overt scares. AI recommends focusing on the unknown to heighten tension.
    - It by Stephen King blends cosmic horror with deeply personal fears, making the story resonate on multiple levels.

5. Literary Fiction
The Promise: "You'll explore complex characters, relationships, and themes that make you reflect on the human condition."

Readers of literary fiction value depth, nuance, and prose that feels as much an art form as the story itself.
- Key AI Insights:
    - Emotional Resonance: AI identifies that successful literary fiction often evokes strong emotional reactions by focusing on deeply human experiences.
    - Subtext: Readers appreciate subtlety. AI suggests refining scenes to leave room for interpretation, rather than spelling out every meaning.
- What Works and Why:
    - The Road by Cormac McCarthy pairs sparse prose with universal themes of hope and despair, making its emotional impact unforgettable. AI highlights the importance of restraint in literary fiction.
    - Americanah by Chimamanda Ngozi Adichie uses a personal love story to explore broader themes of race, identity, and belonging, balancing individual and universal resonance.

How to Exceed Genre Expectations
- Understand Before You Innovate:
    - Master the conventions of your genre before subverting them. Readers need a foundation of familiarity before they can appreciate creative twists.
- Example: Andy Weir's The Martian delivers hard sci-fi rooted in scientific accuracy, but its humor and character-driven approach elevate it beyond genre norms.
- Focus on Emotional Impact:
    - No matter the genre, readers connect most deeply with stories that make them feel. Ensure your characters' emotional journeys are as compelling as the plot.
- Example: Suzanne Collins' The Hunger Games pairs high-stakes action with Katniss's deeply personal struggles, making her journey relatable and gripping.

- Use AI to Stay Fresh:
  - AI can analyze trends, test unconventional ideas, and help you refine your narrative to align with what readers are craving while staying original.

AI Insights on Current Fiction Trends
The literary landscape is always evolving, influenced by changing reader preferences, societal shifts, and technological advances. What captivated audiences a decade ago may not have the same appeal today. To craft stories that feel fresh and relevant, it's important to understand emerging trends and how they align with your creative vision.

AI offers unique tools to help writers stay ahead of the curve by analyzing patterns in bestselling books, reader reviews, and narrative structures. By tapping into these insights, you can identify what resonates most with modern readers and refine your story to stand out in a competitive market.

How AI Identifies Fiction Trends
AI excels at analyzing large datasets to uncover what readers are currently engaging with and why. Here are the key ways AI can provide actionable insights:

- Genre Preferences:
  - AI tracks shifts in reader interest across genres, highlighting rising trends such as the resurgence of gothic horror or the increasing popularity of character-driven science fiction.
- Emerging Themes:
  - AI identifies recurring themes in successful books, such as resilience, personal transformation, or the moral complexities of power and ambition.
- Narrative Techniques:
  - By studying pacing, point of view, and plot structures, AI pinpoints storytelling techniques that are engaging contemporary readers. For instance, nonlinear narratives and dual timelines have gained traction in many genres.
- Audience Feedback:
  - AI tools analyze reader reviews to highlight what audiences love or dislike about specific books, offering insights into pacing, character development, or endings.

Emerging Trends in Fiction
Here are some of the current trends AI has identified as particularly influential across genres:

1. Moral Ambiguity and Complex Characters:
   - Readers are increasingly drawn to characters with layered motivations and flaws. The classic "hero" archetype is evolving into protagonists who make morally complex decisions, reflecting real-world challenges.
   - Example: Kaz Brekker in Leigh Bardugo's Six of Crows is a cunning antihero whose actions are driven by survival, loyalty, and revenge, creating a compelling blend of ruthlessness and vulnerability.

2. Blurring of Genre Boundaries:
   - Books that blend elements from multiple genres, such as romance-infused thrillers or science fiction with mystery elements, are captivating readers looking for unique and unpredictable experiences.
   - Example: Erin Morgenstern's The Night Circus weaves fantasy, romance, and historical fiction into an enchanting narrative that defies traditional genre categorization.

3. Focus on Psychological Depth:
   - Stories that explore inner conflicts, personal growth, or the effects of trauma are resonating deeply with readers. This trend is especially prominent in literary fiction, thrillers, and contemporary dramas.
   - Example: A Man Called Ove by Fredrik Backman offers a heartwarming and deeply psychological exploration of grief, connection, and healing.

4. Cli-Fi and Eco-Fiction:
   - As environmental concerns become more prominent globally, fiction that integrates ecological themes—whether speculative or contemporary—is gaining attention.
   - Example: Richard Powers's The Overstory uses interconnected narratives to explore humanity's relationship with nature, creating a powerful and timely story.

5. Focus on Mental Health and Personal Growth:
   - Fiction exploring mental health challenges or themes of self-discovery continues to grow, particularly in YA and contemporary genres.
   - Example: Eleanor Oliphant Is Completely Fine by Gail Honeyman addresses loneliness and personal healing, resonating with readers seeking emotional connection.

Using AI to Align with Trends Without Losing Originality
While staying aware of trends can help you connect with contemporary readers, originality is key to standing out. Here's how AI can help you achieve both:

1. Analyze Trends Without Copying:
   - Use AI to identify the elements driving current trends (e.g., strong female protagonists or dual timelines) and incorporate them in ways that feel authentic to your story.
2. Test Your Story's Appeal:
   - AI tools can analyze your synopsis, characters, and themes to predict how well your story aligns with reader preferences while offering suggestions for enhancement.
3. Find Your Niche:
   - Instead of chasing trends, AI can help you carve out a unique space by combining popular elements with your distinct voice and vision.

Conclusion: Harnessing AI to Master Genre and Trends
Writing stories that resonate with readers requires more than creativity—it demands an understanding of genre expectations and the evolving literary landscape. Genres provide a framework, offering readers the experience they crave while leaving room for your unique voice. AI enhances this process by analyzing successful books, identifying trends like morally complex characters and experimental storytelling, and helping you craft works that feel both relevant and original.

Great storytelling is about balance: meeting audience expectations while surprising them with fresh perspectives. With AI as your collaborator, you can refine pacing, themes, and characters, aligning your story with reader preferences without compromising your vision. Mastering genre conventions and staying aware of trends aren't constraints—they're opportunities to connect emotionally with readers and leave your mark on the ever-changing world of fiction. Step boldly into this partnership with AI, and let your creativity shine.

Chapter 5: Understanding Genre Tropes and Expectations

Recognizing and Subverting Tropes

Tropes are the building blocks of storytelling. They're familiar ideas, archetypes, and narrative devices that have been used time and again to create compelling tales. Every genre has its own set of tropes—common elements that readers expect and often enjoy. However, tropes can be a double-edged sword: while they provide a sense of familiarity, overused or poorly executed tropes can feel stale or predictable.

To craft a story that resonates with readers, it's important to understand the tropes of your chosen genre and learn how to use, twist, or completely subvert them. This section explores how to recognize tropes, when to lean into them, and how to surprise your audience by breaking the mold.

What Are Tropes?

Tropes are recurring patterns in storytelling that help convey meaning quickly. They can include character types, plot devices, or settings that readers instinctively recognize. For example:

- The Chosen One: A protagonist destined for greatness (Harry Potter, The Matrix).
- The Love Triangle: Two potential romantic interests vying for one character (Twilight, The Hunger Games).
- The Mentor's Sacrifice: A wise mentor who dies to inspire the hero (Star Wars, The Lion King).

Tropes exist because they work—they evoke emotions and create connections with readers. Recognizing and understanding them is the first step to using them effectively.

Why Do Readers Love Tropes?

Tropes create a sense of familiarity, helping readers quickly orient themselves within the story. They provide a framework that allows writers to explore deeper themes or add complexity to their characters and plots. For instance:

- Comfort: Readers enjoy the predictability of certain tropes, like a guaranteed happy ending in romance.
- Efficiency: Tropes allow writers to establish context quickly, leaving more room to develop unique elements.
- Emotional Impact: Tropes tap into universal human experiences, like the desire for belonging or the triumph of good over evil.

Example: The trope of "enemies-to-lovers" in romance consistently appeals to readers because it creates natural tension and emotional payoff when the characters finally reconcile their differences.

Recognizing Tropes in Your Genre
Each genre comes with its own set of established tropes. Here are some common examples:

- Mystery/Thriller:
  - The Red Herring: A false clue that misleads the protagonist (and the reader).
  - The Detective with a Troubled Past: A sleuth driven by personal demons (Sherlock Holmes, True Detective).
- Fantasy:
  - The Prophecy: A foretold event that drives the protagonist's journey (Percy Jackson, The Wheel of Time).
  - The Quest: A journey to achieve a goal, often involving a group of companions (The Hobbit, The Lord of the Rings).
- Science Fiction:
  - The AI Gone Rogue: Technology turning against its creators (Ex Machina, I, Robot).
  - The Dystopian Society: A future world defined by oppression (The Hunger Games, 1984).
- Romance:
  - The Meet-Cute: A quirky or humorous first meeting between romantic leads (You've Got Mail, The Hating Game).
  - The Misunderstanding: A conflict caused by a lack of communication (Pride and Prejudice, Bridgerton).
- Horror:
  - The Haunted House: A setting filled with supernatural or psychological terrors (The Haunting of Hill House, The Shining).
  - The Final Girl: A lone survivor who defeats the villain (Halloween, Scream).

By identifying the tropes that define your genre, you can decide whether to embrace them, reimagine them, or challenge them altogether.

Subverting Tropes: Surprising Your Audience
Readers love tropes, but they also love to be surprised. Subverting a trope means taking something familiar and twisting it in an unexpected way. This keeps your story fresh while still satisfying the emotional needs associated with the trope.

How to Subvert Tropes Effectively
Change the Context:
- Take a familiar trope and place it in an unexpected setting or situation.
- Example: In The Hunger Games, the "dystopian rebellion" trope is given new life by centering it on a survival game show where the rebellion is sparked reluctantly by the protagonist.

Invert the Trope:
- Flip the expectations entirely.
- Example: In Frozen, Disney subverts the "true love's kiss" trope by making the act of true love a sister's sacrifice instead of a romantic gesture.

Add Complexity:
- Layer additional motivations or outcomes onto a trope to make it more nuanced.
- Example: Game of Thrones takes the "hero's journey" trope and complicates it with morally ambiguous characters and unexpected deaths, creating an unpredictable narrative.

Comment on the Trope Itself:
- Use the trope while acknowledging its clichés or limitations.
- Example: Shrek humorously deconstructs fairy tale tropes while still delivering a heartfelt story.

Balancing Familiarity and Innovation
When subverting tropes, it's important to balance innovation with familiarity. If you stray too far from audience expectations, readers may feel disconnected. However, if you lean too heavily on well-worn clichés, your story risks feeling unoriginal.

Honor the Emotional Core: Even when subverting a trope, ensure that the emotional payoff remains intact.
- Example: In Knives Out, the "whodunit" trope is subverted by revealing the culprit early on, but the story still delivers suspense and satisfaction by layering unexpected twists.

Surprise Without Confusion: Make your subversions clear and intentional, so readers appreciate the twist rather than feeling lost or misled.
- Example: The Last Jedi subverts the "heroic mentor" trope by presenting a reluctant, flawed Luke Skywalker, which polarized fans but added depth to the character.

Exercise: Tropes in Your Story
- Identify three tropes commonly used in your genre. Write them down.
- Brainstorm two ways to use each trope in its traditional form and one way to subvert it.
- Example: In a fantasy story, the "chosen one" trope could be:
  o Traditional: A young farmhand discovers they are destined to defeat the dark lord.
  o Subverted: The chosen one fails, and a supporting character must rise to save the day.

Common Pitfalls in Genre Writing
Writing within a genre can be a double-edged sword. While genres provide a framework that helps you connect with readers, they also come with potential traps that can make your story feel clichéd, predictable, or disconnected. To craft compelling, memorable works, it's important to recognize these common pitfalls and learn how to avoid them.

1. Overusing Tropes Without Adding Freshness
Tropes are useful storytelling tools, but over-relying on them without innovation can make your story feel stale. Readers want familiar elements, but they also crave originality that sets your work apart.

Pitfall in Action:
- The Chosen One: A young, reluctant hero discovers they're destined to save the world. This trope has been used countless times in fantasy, from The Lord of the Rings to Harry Potter. Without a unique twist, it risks feeling formulaic.
How to Avoid It:
- Add layers of complexity or subvert the trope to surprise readers.
- Example: In The Broken Earth trilogy by N.K. Jemisin, the "chosen one" trope is reframed through a morally ambiguous protagonist in a world shaped by oppression and survival.

2. Ignoring Reader Expectations
While innovation is essential, straying too far from genre conventions can alienate your audience. Readers pick up a book expecting certain emotional beats or narrative structures, and failing to deliver them can leave them unsatisfied.

Pitfall in Action:
- A romance novel without a satisfying emotional payoff, such as a happy or hopeful ending, can frustrate readers who expect the resolution to be emotionally rewarding.

How to Avoid It:
- Build tension and misdirection through foreshadowing, but ensure twists are earned and consistent with the story.
- Example: In The Silent Patient by Alex Michaelides, the twist is both shocking and deeply tied to the protagonist's psychology, creating an unforgettable payoff.

4. Neglecting Emotional Depth

Some genre stories focus so heavily on plot or world-building that they forget the importance of emotional connection. Readers may enjoy the spectacle of a story but feel unsatisfied if they can't connect with the characters on a personal level.

Pitfall in Action:
- A science fiction novel with intricate world-building but flat, one-dimensional characters risks losing reader engagement.

How to Avoid It:
- Focus on your characters' motivations, desires, and emotional growth. Tie their personal stakes to the larger narrative.
- Example: In Dune by Frank Herbert, the richly developed world is complemented by Paul Atreides' personal journey of loss, duty, and power.

5. World-Building Overload

In genres like fantasy and science fiction, extensive world-building can become a pitfall when too much detail is dumped on readers at once. Overwhelming exposition can slow the pace and disengage readers.

Pitfall in Action:
- Beginning the story with pages of backstory, history, or technical jargon before introducing the plot or characters.

How to Avoid It:
- Reveal your world gradually, weaving details naturally into the narrative. Focus on what's immediately relevant to the plot and characters.
- Example: A Song of Ice and Fire by George R.R. Martin introduces its complex world through character interactions and events, revealing layers as the story progresses.

6. Failing to Innovate

Genres thrive on innovation, and stories that follow conventions too rigidly risk being dismissed as unoriginal. Readers want something that feels fresh, even if it uses familiar elements.

Pitfall in Action:
- A horror story that relies solely on jump scares and clichés (e.g., the haunted house with creaky floors and shadowy figures) without adding depth or new ideas.

How to Avoid It:
- Add unique perspectives, themes, or twists that set your story apart from others in the genre.
- Example: The Haunting of Hill House by Shirley Jackson explores psychological and supernatural horror, blending them seamlessly with themes of isolation and trauma.

7. Overcomplicating the Narrative
Trying to stand out by overloading the plot with twists, subplots, or world-building can make your story confusing or inaccessible to readers.

Pitfall in Action:
- A mystery novel with too many suspects, red herrings, and plot threads that never converge or resolve cleanly.

How to Avoid It:
- Simplify the core story while ensuring each subplot contributes to the main narrative. Clarity and focus are key.
- Example: Big Little Lies by Liane Moriarty juggles multiple subplots but ties them together through a single, compelling central mystery.

Exercise: Spotting and Avoiding Pitfalls
- Choose a Genre: Identify a genre you're writing in and list three common tropes or conventions.
- Analyze Pitfalls: For each trope, consider a potential pitfall.
- Innovate: Brainstorm one way to subvert the trope or add freshness to avoid predictability.
- Example: In a romance, instead of the love triangle trope, consider a scenario where the protagonist discovers self-love and independence as a third option.

Examples from Popular Novels
One of the best ways to master genre tropes and expectations is by studying how successful novels use, subvert, or reinvent them. By analyzing these works, you can gain insights into how to engage readers while adding your unique voice. Let's explore examples from various genres to see how these elements are put into practice.

1. Mystery/Thriller
- Novel: The Girl with the Dragon Tattoo by Stieg Larsson
  - Trope Used: The troubled detective with a dark past.
  - How It Works: Mikael Blomkvist, while not a traditional detective, carries a flawed, deeply human perspective that draws readers into the mystery. This trope creates empathy and adds stakes as the protagonist seeks justice while grappling with personal failures.
  - Twist on Expectations: The unconventional partnership with Lisbeth Salander, a hacker with her own troubled past, subverts the lone-detective archetype, creating a dynamic duo that reinvents the genre.
- Novel: Gone Girl by Gillian Flynn
  - Trope Used: The unreliable narrator.
  - How It Works: Flynn uses alternating perspectives to build suspense and mislead readers. This trope keeps the audience guessing as they piece together the truth.
  - Twist on Expectations: The mid-story reveal flips the narrative on its head, showing how a familiar trope can still feel fresh when executed cleverly.

2. Romance
- Novel: Pride and Prejudice by Jane Austen
  - Trope Used: Enemies-to-lovers.
  - How It Works: Elizabeth Bennet and Mr. Darcy's journey from animosity to mutual admiration provides emotional tension and a satisfying payoff, hallmarks of a strong romance.
  - Twist on Expectations: Austen layers societal critique into the romantic arc, elevating the trope into a commentary on class, gender, and personal growth.
- Novel: The Hating Game by Sally Thorne
  - Trope Used: Workplace rivalry turned romance.
  - How It Works: The playful banter and escalating tension between Lucy and Joshua keep readers invested, fulfilling the emotional highs and lows romance fans expect.
  - Twist on Expectations: Thorne adds depth by exploring themes of self-worth and ambition, making the romance more than just external conflict.

3. Science Fiction/Fantasy

- Novel: Dune by Frank Herbert
  - Trope Used: The hero's journey.
  - How It Works: Paul Atreides's transformation from a reluctant heir to a messianic figure follows the classic hero's arc, a cornerstone of epic storytelling.
  - Twist on Expectations: Herbert complicates the trope by embedding political intrigue, ecological themes, and moral ambiguity, creating a layered narrative that challenges traditional heroic ideals.
- Novel: The Hunger Games by Suzanne Collins
  - Trope Used: The dystopian rebellion.
  - How It Works: Katniss Everdeen embodies the reluctant hero archetype, thrust into a revolution she never sought. This aligns with readers' expectations of resistance against an oppressive regime.
  - Twist on Expectations: The focus on personal stakes, survival, and the psychological toll of rebellion sets this series apart from standard dystopian fare.

4. Horror

- Novel: The Haunting of Hill House by Shirley Jackson
  - Trope Used: The haunted house.
  - How It Works: Hill House is the perfect setting for psychological and supernatural horror, creating a claustrophobic atmosphere that plays on readers' fears.
  - Twist on Expectations: Jackson blurs the line between external and internal horror, leaving readers questioning whether the true menace lies in the house or the characters' minds.
- Novel: It by Stephen King
  - Trope Used: The small-town terror.
  - How It Works: King uses the familiar trope of an idyllic town hiding dark secrets to create a chilling narrative. The alternating timelines build suspense and deepen the stakes.
  - Twist on Expectations: The villain, Pennywise, embodies both supernatural terror and the fears of childhood, making the horror personal and universal.

5. Literary Fiction
- Novel: The Road by Cormac McCarthy
  - Trope Used: The post-apocalyptic journey.
  - How It Works: A father and son's struggle for survival in a bleak, desolate world captures the essence of humanity under duress.
  - Twist on Expectations: McCarthy's sparse prose and focus on the emotional bond between the protagonists elevate the story from survival fiction to a profound meditation on hope and love.
- Novel: Atonement by Ian McEwan
  - Trope Used: The unreliable narrator.
  - How It Works: The story hinges on the subjective perception of events, creating layers of tension and tragedy.
  - Twist on Expectations: The novel's ending reframes the entire narrative, revealing the narrator's guilt and the unreliability of memory.

Why These Examples Work
Each of these novels uses familiar tropes as a foundation but elevates them through innovation, complexity, and emotional depth. By studying how these works balance convention and creativity, you can gain valuable insights into crafting stories that meet reader expectations while offering something uniquely yours.

Exercise: Applying Lessons from Popular Novels
- Choose one of your favorite novels from your genre.
- Identify the main trope it uses.
- Reflect on how the author executes or subverts the trope.
- Brainstorm ways you could use the same trope in your story while adding your unique twist.

Conclusion: Mastering Genre Tropes and Expectations
Understanding genre tropes and expectations is about more than just following established patterns—it's about learning to wield them effectively. Tropes are powerful tools that connect your story to readers by tapping into familiar emotional beats and narrative structures. By recognizing these elements and knowing when to embrace, twist, or subvert them, you can create a story that feels both satisfying and fresh.

However, writing within a genre comes with its challenges. Common pitfalls, such as over-relying on predictable tropes, neglecting emotional depth, or overwhelming readers with excessive exposition, can undermine even the most promising story. By identifying these pitfalls and learning how to avoid them, you can ensure your narrative remains engaging and true to your creative vision. Remember, balance is key: give readers what they love while surprising them with unique twists that only you can bring to the genre.

The best lessons come from studying successful novels. Great authors use genre conventions as a foundation while elevating their stories with innovation, complexity, and emotional resonance. Whether it's the subversion of the haunted house trope in The Haunting of Hill House, the reimagining of the dystopian rebellion in The Hunger Games, or the layered moral ambiguity in Gone Girl, these works showcase how to exceed reader expectations while staying rooted in genre traditions.

As you move forward, think of genre tropes and expectations not as limitations but as opportunities. Use them to anchor your story while exploring the edges of possibility. Let the pitfalls become checkpoints that guide you toward stronger storytelling, and let the examples from successful works inspire you to push your creativity further. By mastering these elements, you'll craft stories that resonate, entertain, and stand out in a crowded literary landscape.

Your genre is a canvas—paint it boldly.

Chapter 6: Building Memorable Characters

How to Create Complex, Believable Characters

At the heart of every great story are characters who feel real—people who breathe life into the narrative and linger in the reader's mind long after the final page. Complex, believable characters draw readers in by reflecting the contradictions, emotions, and struggles we all experience. They're not just vehicles for the plot; they are the story.

In this section, we'll explore how to craft multidimensional characters and analyze examples of some of the most compelling characters in literature to understand why they work so well.

1. What Makes a Character Complex and Believable?

Believable characters possess a mix of traits, flaws, desires, and conflicts that make them feel human. Complexity arises when characters defy easy categorization, showing layers of behavior and motivation that evolve throughout the story.

Key traits of complex characters include:
- Goals and Motivations: Characters should want something and have reasons for wanting it, whether it's love, revenge, or survival.
- Flaws and Contradictions: Real people aren't perfect, and believable characters shouldn't be either. Contradictions make them more relatable.
- Depth and Backstory: Past experiences shape a character's present decisions, adding depth to their actions.
- Change Over Time: A static character often feels flat. Believable characters grow, adapt, and reveal new facets of themselves as the story unfolds.

2. Drawing Inspiration from Great Characters

Let's analyze some iconic characters to uncover the secrets behind their believability and complexity:

Elizabeth Bennet – Pride and Prejudice by Jane Austen
- Why She Works: Elizabeth is intelligent, witty, and fiercely independent, but her pride and quick judgments often cloud her perception of others. Her flaws and eventual self-awareness make her relatable and endearing.
- Lesson: Balance strengths with weaknesses to create a well-rounded character. Let flaws drive conflict and growth.

Jay Gatsby – The Great Gatsby by F. Scott Fitzgerald
- Why He Works: Gatsby is enigmatic and ambitious, driven by his obsessive love for Daisy and his desire to reinvent himself. His mysterious past and relentless hope clash with the emptiness of his reality, making him a tragic figure.
- Lesson: Ambiguity can make a character compelling. Let their secrets unravel slowly, revealing depth and complexity.

Katniss Everdeen – The Hunger Games by Suzanne Collins
- Why She Works: Katniss is a reluctant hero, motivated by survival and her love for her family rather than any noble cause. Her resourcefulness and emotional vulnerability make her relatable, even in extraordinary circumstances.
- Lesson: Ground characters in personal stakes and emotions, even in high-concept settings.

Walter White – Breaking Bad (TV)
- Why He Works: Walter begins as a sympathetic, mild-mannered chemistry teacher but gradually transforms into a ruthless drug lord. His decisions are driven by a mix of desperation, pride, and a need for control, making him both relatable and horrifying.
- Lesson: Explore moral ambiguity and let characters evolve in unexpected ways, reflecting both their choices and external pressures.

Offred – The Handmaid's Tale by Margaret Atwood
- Why She Works: Offred is a passive observer in a dystopian world, but her inner life is rich with memory, rebellion, and longing. Her quiet defiance and moments of vulnerability make her deeply human.
- Lesson: Use internal conflict and rich inner monologues to create depth, especially for characters in restrictive environments.

Holden Caulfield – The Catcher in the Rye by J.D. Salinger
- Why He Works: Holden's cynicism and alienation resonate with readers because they reflect universal feelings of uncertainty and fear during adolescence. His contradictions—sensitivity masked by bitterness—make him relatable.
- Lesson: Tap into universal emotions like loneliness or identity struggles to connect characters to readers.

3. Practical Techniques for Crafting Complex Characters
To create characters as compelling as those above, consider these practical techniques:

1. Develop Detailed Backstories
   - Why It Matters: A character's past influences their present. Knowing their history, even if it isn't all revealed in the story, helps you write them authentically.
   - Example: Jay Gatsby's mysterious past shapes his relentless pursuit of Daisy and his extravagant lifestyle.
2. Use Contradictions
   - Why It Matters: Contradictions make characters feel real. A brave character might have moments of doubt, or a kind character might act selfishly under pressure.
   - Example: Katniss Everdeen is a skilled hunter but struggles with expressing her emotions.
3. Give Them Goals and Flaws
   - Why It Matters: Believable characters want something (a goal) and face obstacles (internal or external) that make achieving it difficult.
   - Example: Elizabeth Bennet's quick judgments and pride initially blind her to Darcy's true character.
4. Show, Don't Tell
   - Why It Matters: Actions and choices reveal character more effectively than exposition.
   - Example: Offred's quiet acts of rebellion in The Handmaid's Tale show her resistance without her needing to state it outright.
5. Allow Characters to Change
   - Why It Matters: Growth and transformation keep characters dynamic and engaging.
   - Example: Walter White's descent into villainy is both shocking and inevitable, making his transformation gripping.
6. Leverage Internal Conflict
   - Why It Matters: Characters who wrestle with internal struggles feel more relatable.
   - Example: Holden Caulfield's inner turmoil reflects the universal challenge of finding one's place in the world.

Exercise: Build Your Own Complex Character
- Backstory: Write a one-paragraph summary of your character's past. What key events shaped them?
- Strengths and Flaws: List three strengths and three flaws. How do these traits interact to create tension?
- Goals and Obstacles: Identify what your character wants most and the internal/external challenges preventing them from achieving it.
- Contradictions: Choose one way your character acts unpredictably. How does this contradiction add depth?
- Emotional Growth: Outline how your character will change by the end of the story.

Character Arcs: Growth and Transformation
Great stories are driven by characters who change. A well-crafted character arc takes your protagonist on a journey, whether it's a journey of self-discovery, a descent into darkness, or a transformation shaped by external challenges. Readers are drawn to arcs because they mirror the human experience—growth, failure, resilience, and change.

In this section, we'll explore the different types of character arcs, their key components, and how well-known characters demonstrate growth and transformation.

1. What Is a Character Arc?
A character arc is the transformation or inner journey a character undergoes over the course of a story. Arcs add depth and meaning to your narrative, giving readers a reason to root for, question, or reflect on the character.

Key Elements of a Character Arc:
- The Starting Point: Who is your character at the beginning of the story? What are their flaws, desires, or misconceptions?
- Challenges and Growth: What obstacles force the character to change or grow?
- The Transformation: How is your character different by the end of the story? Did they overcome their flaws, fail spectacularly, or find a balance?

2. Types of Character Arcs
Let's examine the three most common types of character arcs, with examples from popular stories.

A. Positive Change Arc
In a positive arc, the character grows or transforms for the better, overcoming internal or external challenges to achieve their goals.
- Example 1: Elizabeth Bennet in Pride and Prejudice*
    - Starting Point: Elizabeth begins the story as intelligent and independent but quick to judge and overly proud.
    - Challenges: Her encounters with Mr. Darcy force her to confront her own flaws, including her prejudices and assumptions.
    - Transformation: By the end of the story, Elizabeth gains self-awareness, humility, and a deeper understanding of herself and others, paving the way for her relationship with Darcy.
    - Why It Works: Readers relate to Elizabeth's flaws and celebrate her growth, which feels authentic and earned.
- Example 2: Bilbo Baggins in The Hobbit*
    - Starting Point: Bilbo is timid, reluctant to leave the safety of the Shire, and unsure of his own capabilities.
    - Challenges: His journey with the dwarves tests his courage and resourcefulness.
    - Transformation: By the end of the story, Bilbo becomes a braver, wiser, and more self-assured individual who has discovered his own inner strength.
    - Why It Works: Bilbo's gradual growth, driven by external challenges and internal resolve, is both satisfying and relatable.

B. Negative Change Arc
In a negative arc, the character's flaws deepen, or they descend into darkness due to their choices or circumstances.
- Example 1: Walter White in Breaking Bad*
    - Starting Point: Walter begins as a mild-mannered chemistry teacher who justifies his entry into the drug trade as a way to support his family.
    - Challenges: As his success grows, his pride and lust for power overshadow his initial intentions.
    - Transformation: By the end of the series, Walter has become a ruthless criminal mastermind, alienating everyone he once cared about.
    - Why It Works: Walter's descent is gradual, logical, and deeply tied to his motivations, making it both horrifying and compelling.

- Example 2: Anakin Skywalker in the Star Wars Prequels*
  - Starting Point: Anakin begins as a gifted and idealistic Jedi with dreams of bringing peace to the galaxy.
  - Challenges: His fear of loss, manipulation by Palpatine, and growing power lead him to betray his values.
  - Transformation: By the end, Anakin becomes Darth Vader, a tragic figure consumed by his ambition and insecurities.
  - Why It Works: Anakin's arc resonates because it shows how fear and pride can corrupt even the most promising individuals.

C. Flat (or Static) Arc
In a flat arc, the character remains steadfast in their beliefs and values, inspiring change in the world or other characters around them.
- Example 1: Atticus Finch in To Kill a Mockingbird*
  - Starting Point: Atticus is a principled lawyer who believes in justice and equality.
  - Challenges: He faces prejudice, hostility, and danger while defending Tom Robinson, a Black man falsely accused of a crime.
  - Transformation: Atticus's core values remain unchanged, but his courage and integrity inspire growth in his children, particularly Scout.
  - Why It Works: Atticus serves as a moral anchor, demonstrating the power of standing by one's principles.
- Example 2: Katniss Everdeen in The Hunger Games*
  - Starting Point: Katniss is a survivor, fiercely protective of her family and unwilling to be a pawn in the Capitol's games.
  - Challenges: Despite being thrust into life-threatening situations, Katniss remains true to her values and becomes a symbol of rebellion.
  - Transformation: While Katniss herself doesn't change drastically, her actions ignite change in Panem, making her a catalyst for revolution.
  - Why It Works: Flat arcs work well for protagonists who inspire change in others rather than undergoing significant growth themselves.

3. Crafting a Powerful Character Arc

To create an impactful arc, consider these steps:

- Define the Starting Point: Who is your character at the beginning? What flaws, beliefs, or goals shape them?
- Example: At the start of The Catcher in the Rye, Holden Caulfield is disillusioned and struggling to find meaning.
- Plan the Turning Points: Identify key moments that challenge your character's beliefs or force them to grow.
- Example: In The Hunger Games, Katniss's decision to risk her life for her sister is a defining moment that reveals her courage and selflessness.
- End with Transformation: How has your character changed by the end? If they haven't changed, how has their presence influenced others?
- Example: In The Great Gatsby, Gatsby's arc ends in tragedy, reflecting the futility of his relentless pursuit of the past.

Exercise: Create a Character Arc

- Starting Point: Write a brief description of who your character is at the beginning of the story.
- Challenges: List three key challenges or events that will force them to grow or change.
- Transformation: Describe how your character will be different by the end of the story.
- Alignment: Identify whether your character's arc is positive, negative, or flat.

Conclusion: Crafting Characters That Captivate

Memorable characters are at the heart of every great story. They breathe life into your narrative, forge emotional connections with readers, and drive the plot forward in ways only they can. By focusing on creating complex, believable characters, you ensure your protagonists, antagonists, and even minor players feel like real people with strengths, flaws, and contradictions that resonate.

But character creation is just the beginning. A well-crafted character arc transforms those believable figures into dynamic forces within your story. Whether they experience positive growth, tragic decline, or serve as a steadfast anchor inspiring change in others, character arcs provide the emotional depth and evolution that keep readers engaged. The transformation—or lack of it—mirrors the human experience, making your story feel authentic and meaningful.

By studying examples of iconic characters like Elizabeth Bennet, Walter White, and Katniss Everdeen, you can learn how to balance familiarity with innovation, creating characters who feel fresh yet relatable. Whether through a flawed hero's redemption, a villain's descent into darkness, or a steadfast figure's impact on their world, your characters' journeys can become the driving force that keeps readers turning pages.

As you develop your own characters, remember: the key is to make them human. Give them contradictions, let them grow (or fail), and tie their inner struggles to the larger themes of your story. When your characters feel alive, your readers won't just follow your story —they'll live it.

Chapter 7: Using AI to Expand and Enhance Story Ideas

AI isn't just a tool—it's your creative mentor, helping you unlock the ideas, characters, and plot twists already waiting in your mind. Instead of replacing your creativity, AI amplifies it, offering guidance, fresh perspectives, and structured techniques to bring out the best in your storytelling.

In this chapter, we'll explore how to use AI to generate character profiles, uncover surprising plot twists, and overcome creative blocks. Along the way, we'll discuss proven techniques from famous writers and show how AI can guide you to explore new directions in your work.

1. Generating Character Profiles and Plot Twists

Well-rounded characters and unexpected plot twists are the lifeblood of great stories. AI can help you refine your characters and develop twists that feel both surprising and inevitable—reflecting ideas you might not have realized were already there.

How AI Helps Generate Character Profiles
AI can guide you through the process of creating multidimensional characters by asking the right questions. Instead of presenting you with ready-made ideas, AI acts as a brainstorming partner, helping you dig deeper into your characters' backstories, motivations, and relationships.
Example Technique: The "Why, Why, Why?" Method

- Famous writers like J.K. Rowling have emphasized the importance of understanding why your characters act as they do. AI can help by prompting questions:
  - Why does your protagonist want this goal?
  - Why is this goal important to their backstory?
  - Why will this goal create conflict with others in the story?

Practical AI Tip: Use AI to build layered profiles by inputting basic traits (e.g., "a shy librarian with a secret love for adventure") and asking for prompts about fears, flaws, dreams, and contradictions. These responses can spark ideas you hadn't considered.

How AI Helps Create Plot Twists
Plot twists succeed when they feel both surprising and inevitable—moments that make readers think, "Of course! How did I miss that?" AI can help by analyzing your story setup and suggesting twists that fit logically within your world and characters.

Example Technique: The Chekhov's Gun Principle
- Anton Chekhov famously said, "If in the first act you have hung a pistol on the wall, then in the following one it should be fired." Effective plot twists often emerge from seeds planted earlier in the story.
  - AI can help you identify elements you've introduced—minor characters, objects, or events—and brainstorm ways to give them greater significance later.

Example: In Agatha Christie's The Murder of Roger Ackroyd, the twist works because the clues were subtly present throughout the story, rewarding attentive readers. AI can analyze your draft and suggest ways to enhance foreshadowing for similar impact.

2. Overcoming Creative Blocks
Every writer faces creative blocks, but AI can act as a coach to guide you through them. Whether you're stuck on a scene, unsure how to transition between chapters, or struggling with a subplot, AI provides prompts and strategies to reignite your creativity.
How AI Helps with Writer's Block
- Scenario-Based Prompts: If you're stuck, AI can suggest scenarios to move your story forward.
- Example: "What happens if your protagonist discovers a hidden letter in their nemesis's home?"

- Shifting Perspectives: AI can encourage you to view the story from another character's perspective, revealing hidden opportunities for tension or insight.
- Example: Rewrite a pivotal scene from the antagonist's point of view to discover motivations or conflicts you hadn't explored.

Techniques from Famous Writers for Breaking Through Blocks
A. The "What If?" Technique
Stephen King often uses "What if?" scenarios to generate ideas and overcome stagnation. AI can help you brainstorm:
What if your protagonist's closest ally is secretly working against them?
What if a minor detail in the setting becomes pivotal to the plot?

B. Freewriting
Writers like Natalie Goldberg advocate for freewriting to unlock subconscious ideas. AI can assist by providing starting points or random prompts to spark ideas.

C. The Hemingway Rule

Ernest Hemingway believed in ending each writing session mid-sentence to make it easier to pick up the next day. AI can help by suggesting where to leave off or providing questions to focus on when you return.

3. Exploring New Directions

Sometimes, the best stories emerge when you take your narrative in unexpected directions. AI can inspire you to experiment with "what if" scenarios, alternate endings, or even shifts in genre or tone, helping you explore possibilities you might not have considered.

How AI Encourages Fresh Perspectives
- Alternate Outcomes: AI can suggest alternate resolutions for key scenes to explore how they change the story.

- Example: What happens if the villain succeeds in Act Two, forcing the protagonist to regroup and find a new approach?
- Genre Shifts: AI can help you reimagine your story in a different genre, giving it a fresh angle.
- Example: Rewriting a mystery subplot as a romantic revelation could uncover new emotional stakes.

Techniques for Expanding Ideas

1. Reverse the Expected
- Many writers, including Neil Gaiman, advocate for subverting clichés. AI can help you brainstorm inversions of common tropes:
  o Instead of the hero triumphing, what if they fail spectacularly and have to rebuild?
  o Instead of a villain's defeat, what if they manipulate the protagonist into helping them?

2. Character-Driven Twists
- Some of the best plot developments arise from character choices. AI can suggest conflicts that challenge your characters' goals and values:
- Example: If your character's greatest fear comes true, how would they react?

3. Parallel Timelines
- Authors like Emily St. John Mandel (Station Eleven) use nonlinear storytelling to add depth. AI can brainstorm alternate timelines or flashbacks to enrich your narrative.

Exercise: Let AI Help You Brainstorm
- Character Development: Use AI to generate a 5-question interview for your protagonist. Answer the questions in their voice to uncover hidden motivations or contradictions.
- Plot Twists: Input a basic plot summary and ask AI to suggest three potential twists. Choose one and refine it, ensuring it aligns with your story's logic.
- Breaking a Block: Describe a scene you're struggling with and let AI suggest three ways to resolve it. Freewrite from one of those ideas for 10 minutes.

Conclusion: AI as a Creative Mentor
AI is more than a tool—it's a collaborative partner that helps you unlock the ideas already waiting inside your mind. By guiding you through character development, plot twists, and creative blocks, AI amplifies your storytelling instincts, encouraging you to take risks and explore new possibilities. The best stories come from within, and with AI as your mentor, you can bring those stories to life in ways that feel authentic, surprising, and uniquely yours.

Chapter 8: Character-Driven Storytelling

Crafting Relationships and Emotional Depth
Relationships are the beating heart of any character-driven story. Whether built on love, rivalry, mutual respect, or bitter enmity, relationships define your characters and drive your plot forward. They connect readers to your story, raise the stakes, and deepen emotional engagement. Relationships give readers a reason to care, to root for resolution, or to anticipate conflict.

At their core, meaningful relationships feel authentic because they reflect the complexity of human connections. These relationships evolve over time, are driven by shared experiences or conflicts, and allow both characters to grow. By analyzing successful stories, AI has highlighted key trends in crafting compelling relationships:

- Emotional Authenticity: Relationships resonate when characters' emotions—love, hate, trust, betrayal—feel real and earned.
- Dynamic Evolution: The best relationships aren't static. They evolve, for better or worse, as characters face external pressures or internal revelations.
- Conflict and Tension: Relationships don't have to be friendly to be compelling. Rivalries, grudges, and unlikely partnerships often create the most engaging dynamics.

In this section, we'll explore the key elements of strong relationships, how they evolve, and the nuances that make them memorable across genres. We'll draw on famous examples and AI insights to help you create dynamic, emotionally resonant relationships in your own storytelling.

1. Key Elements of Strong Relationships

A. Shared History and Emotional Anchors
A sense of shared history, even if not fully revealed to the reader, adds depth and believability to relationships. These histories can be rooted in love, loyalty, trauma, or conflict.

- Example 1: Frodo and Sam – The Lord of the Rings
    - Why It Works: Sam's unwavering loyalty to Frodo is grounded in years of trust and friendship. Sam acts as Frodo's emotional and moral anchor as the burden of the One Ring threatens to break him.
    - Takeaway: Create characters who support each other in complementary ways, highlighting devotion and resilience.

- Example 2: Arya Stark and The Hound – Game of Thrones
  - Why It Works: Initially defined by disdain, their relationship evolves as they endure shared dangers. The grudging respect that develops feels earned because of the hardships they face together.
  - Takeaway: Implied backstories and shared challenges can transform hostile dynamics into compelling bonds.

B. Conflict and Resolution
Conflict tests relationships, revealing character flaws and strengths. Whether resolved or not, these struggles create emotional tension that engages readers.

- Example 1: Elizabeth Bennet & Mr. Darcy – Pride & Prejudice
  - Why It Works: Their relationship thrives on misjudgment and misunderstanding, which they must overcome to develop mutual respect and love. Their flaws—Elizabeth's prejudice and Darcy's pride—drive the conflict and its eventual resolution.
  - Takeaway: Build relationships where characters challenge each other, forcing growth through conflict.
- Example 2: Walter White and Jesse Pinkman – Breaking Bad
  - Why It Works: Their toxic, co-dependent relationship adds layers to the narrative. While Walter often manipulates Jesse, their shared experiences create a bond that is deeply human yet destructive.
  - Takeaway: Not all relationships need to be healthy to be compelling. Conflict can highlight moral complexities and power dynamics.

C. Vulnerability and Emotional Depth
Vulnerability invites readers to connect with characters, making relationships feel genuine and impactful.

- Example 1: Katniss and Rue – The Hunger Games
  - Why It Works: Their bond, formed in the deadly arena, highlights themes of innocence and loss. Rue's death serves as a turning point for Katniss, deepening her resolve to fight against the Capitol.
  - Takeaway: Use moments of shared vulnerability to create emotional turning points for your characters.
- Example 2: Sethe and Denver – Beloved by Toni Morrison
  - Why It Works: Denver's unwavering support for her mother, despite the haunting presence of Beloved, underscores themes of familial resilience and sacrifice.
  - Takeaway: Explore relationships that reveal the strength and fragility of family bonds.

2. Genre-Specific Nuances

Relationships adapt to the needs and tone of different genres. Understanding these nuances helps ground your characters within the world of your story.

Thrillers: Relationships Built on Tension
In thrillers, relationships often hinge on mistrust, deception, and hidden agendas.

- Example: Amy and Nick – Gone Girl
  - Why It Works: Their manipulative marriage forms the core of the narrative, with lies and secrets layered in their interactions.
  - Takeaway: Use deception and mistrust to add suspense and keep readers guessing.

Romance: Intimacy and Conflict
Romantic relationships thrive on emotional stakes, gradual growth, and satisfying resolutions.

- Example: Noah and Allie – The Notebook
  - Why It Works: Small, intimate gestures like brushing hair away amplify emotional connection. Their love story is heightened by external conflicts and misunderstandings.
  - Takeaway: Layer moments of intimacy and conflict to deepen the emotional stakes of a romantic relationship.

Fantasy/Adventure: Bonds Forged Through Trials
In fantasy and adventure stories, relationships often evolve through shared danger and moral dilemmas.

- Example: Aragorn and Boromir – The Lord of the Rings
  - Why It Works: Boromir's jealousy and eventual redemption create a complex relationship with Aragorn, shifting from rivalry to respect.
  - Takeaway: Use shared adversity to test relationships, revealing characters' values and priorities.

3. How Relationships Evolve Over Time

Evolving relationships feel authentic because they reflect the fluidity of real human connections. Whether deepened by conflict, shaped by trauma, or fractured by betrayal, these shifts keep readers emotionally invested.

A. Growth Through Conflict
Conflict forces characters to confront their flaws and make choices that reveal their true selves.
- Example: Jamie Lannister and Brienne of Tarth – Game of Thrones
  - Why It Works: Their initial animosity evolves into mutual respect as they endure hardship together. Jamie's vulnerable moments, like confessing his "Kingslayer" story, deepen their bond.
  - Takeaway: Use conflict to drive character growth and transform relationships.

B. Bonds Forged Through Shared Trauma
Adversity often strengthens relationships, revealing who characters can truly rely on.
- Example: Katniss and Rue – The Hunger Games
  - Why It Works: Their bond, formed in the deadly arena, highlights themes of innocence and loss. Rue's death serves as a turning point for Katniss, deepening her resolve to fight against the Capitol.
  - Takeaway: Use moments of shared hardship to deepen relationships, creating emotional turning points for your characters.

C. Fractured Relationships That Reflect Reality
Not all relationships end in reconciliation, and that realism can resonate deeply with readers.
- Example: Amir and Hassan – The Kite Runner
  - Why It Works: Amir's betrayal and guilt shape their relationship, even after Hassan's death. This unresolved conflict drives Amir's quest for redemption.
  - Takeaway: Show the lingering effects of unresolved conflicts to create layered, emotionally rich relationships.

What AI Has Noticed About Relationships
AI analysis of successful stories reveals key trends in crafting relationships:
- Conflict Creates Engagement: Tension and disagreements, even in friendships, make relationships compelling.
  - Example: Arya Stark and The Hound's partnership in Game of Thrones thrives on mutual disdain that evolves into begrudging respect.
- Unconventional Bonds Are Memorable: Relationships that defy traditional tropes, such as mentor-apprentice dynamics or toxic alliances, stand out.
- Change Is Essential: Static relationships lose momentum. Even unresolved conflicts should lead to dynamic shifts over time.

Practical Exercise: Deepening Relationships

- Choose two characters from your story with a key relationship (e.g., friends, rivals, or lovers).
- Write three moments in their shared history that define their connection.
- Brainstorm a scene where this relationship is tested. Focus on the emotional stakes and how the outcome will affect both characters.
- Revise the scene to include physical actions or dialogue that reveal hidden feelings or vulnerabilities.

Dialogue and Body Language

Dialogue and body language are the lifeblood of character interactions. Together, they reveal not only what characters say but also what they mean, what they hide, and how they feel. Mastering these elements allows writers to create scenes that resonate emotionally and feel authentic, capturing the complexity of human behavior.

This section explores how to craft effective dialogue and body language, emphasizing the interplay between them. We'll discuss their role in storytelling, techniques for adding depth and subtext, and how to avoid common pitfalls. Examples from literature and fresh insights will guide you in creating character-driven scenes that engage readers on multiple levels.

1. The Role of Dialogue and Body Language in Storytelling

Dialogue and body language fulfill critical storytelling functions:

- Reveal Character: A character's words and gestures reflect their background, personality, and emotional state. A brash character might dominate conversations, while a reserved one might reveal themselves through subtle movements.
  - Insight: Dialogue shows what a character chooses to say; body language reveals what they can't or won't express.
- Build Subtext: Words and actions often carry unspoken meanings. A forced smile during an apology, for instance, may suggest insincerity.
  - Insight: The tension between spoken words and physical cues creates emotional layers, engaging readers on a deeper level.
- Drive the Plot: Conversations can move the story forward by conveying critical information, escalating conflict, or deepening relationships. Meanwhile, physical reactions emphasize stakes and turning points.
  - Insight: Dialogue and body language together can turn an ordinary exchange into a pivotal moment.

2. Advanced Techniques for Dialogue

A. Creating Emotional Rhythm with Pacing and Tone

The pacing and tone of dialogue can shape a scene's emotional impact. Varying sentence length, rhythm, and word choice allows writers to build tension or intimacy.

Technique 1: Short Sentences for High Stakes
- Short, clipped sentences convey urgency or conflict, mimicking real-life rapid exchanges during tense moments.
    - Example: A frantic argument:
        - "You lied to me."
        - "It wasn't like that—"
        - "Then what was it?"
    - Why It Works: The brevity reflects escalating anger and frustration, immersing readers in the tension.

Technique 2: Long Sentences for Reflection or Intimacy
- Longer, flowing sentences are ideal for contemplative or romantic moments, creating a sense of calm or vulnerability.
    - Example: A quiet confession:
        - "I've spent every day wondering if I could have done something differently—if one word, one choice, could have changed everything."
    - Why It Works: The unbroken rhythm mirrors the speaker's emotional vulnerability, drawing the reader into their thoughts.

B. Building Subtext in Conversations

Subtext allows writers to convey more than what is explicitly stated, adding layers of meaning that engage the reader.

Technique 1: Veiled Criticism
- A character may use politeness to disguise an insult or critique, creating tension without overt conflict.
    - Example:
        - "Your plan is... ambitious. I'm sure it'll be fascinating to see how it turns out."
    - Why It Works: The phrasing suggests support while subtly questioning the plan's feasibility, revealing underlying skepticism.

Technique 2: Emotional Misalignment
- Characters may say one thing but mean another, with their body language exposing the truth.
    - Example: A character says, "I'm fine," while avoiding eye contact and gripping the edge of a table.
    - Why It Works: The contradiction between words and actions hints at deeper, unspoken emotions.

3. Body Language as Silent Dialogue
Sometimes, what a character doesn't say speaks louder than their words. Body language can reveal emotions, highlight power dynamics, or add nuance to relationships.

A. Using Gestures to Enhance Emotion
Technique 1: Small, Intentional Movements
- Small gestures—biting a lip, drumming fingers, or adjusting a collar—can convey nervousness, impatience, or discomfort.
  - Example: A character fidgets with their wedding ring while talking about their spouse, subtly hinting at doubt or guilt.

Technique 2: Larger Physical Reactions
- Sweeping or exaggerated movements can amplify emotions like anger or excitement.
  - Example: A character slams a door after an argument, emphasizing their frustration without needing dialogue.

B. Power Dynamics in Physicality
The way characters occupy physical space reveals power dynamics in a scene.

- Example 1: A commanding character may lean forward during an argument, invading the other person's space, while their counterpart retreats or folds their arms defensively.
- Example 2: A nervous character may glance around the room or shuffle their feet, while a confident one stands tall and still, commanding attention.

Why It Works: These physical contrasts highlight the emotional stakes and relationship dynamics without relying on exposition.

4. Avoiding Forced Exposition
Exposition is necessary for storytelling, but when it's forced into dialogue, it can feel unnatural and clunky.

Common Mistake: Overexplaining
- Example:
  - "As you know, we've been best friends since kindergarten, and you've always been the brave one."
  - Why It Fails: The dialogue exists solely for the reader and doesn't reflect how real people speak.

Solution: Subtle Backstory Through Action and Implied Dialogue
- Fix Example:
  - She smiled faintly, her fingers tracing the edge of the old friendship bracelet. "I think you're braver than you give yourself credit for."
  - Why It Works: The action (tracing the bracelet) hints at their shared history, while the dialogue feels organic and emotionally resonant.

Conclusion: Crafting Meaningful Connections
In this chapter, we've explored the essential elements that make stories resonate: the relationships between characters and the interplay of dialogue and body language. Relationships provide the emotional core of storytelling, connecting readers to your characters and raising the stakes of your narrative. Whether built on love, rivalry, or mutual respect, strong relationships evolve over time, shaped by shared experiences, moments of vulnerability, and conflicts that test their limits.

We delved into the tools that bring relationships to life. Dialogue reveals what characters say and mean, while body language uncovers what they hide or feel but cannot express. Together, these elements build subtext, create emotional depth, and propel the plot forward. From the tension of terse exchanges to the intimacy of reflective confessions, dialogue and physicality allow you to craft moments that feel authentic and emotionally charged.

Relationships and interactions thrive on evolution. They grow through conflict, deepen through shared trauma, or fracture under the weight of betrayal. By weaving these dynamics into your story, you can create connections that are complex and engaging, as seen in iconic pairings like Frodo and Sam or Walter White and Jesse Pinkman. By mastering techniques such as pacing, subtext, and the subtle power of body language, your scenes will resonate with readers and leave a lasting impact.

Through these tools, your storytelling becomes a window into the human experience. With AI as a creative ally, you can refine dialogue, enhance descriptions, and ensure every interaction reflects the emotional authenticity readers crave. Your characters' voices, silences, and gestures will not only shape their relationships but also elevate your story into something readers will cherish long after they've turned the final page.

Chapter 9: Shaping Your Story's DNA

Every story, no matter its genre or complexity, has a unique narrative framework—a structural DNA that determines how it unfolds. Just as the DNA of a living being defines its growth, behavior, and identity, the structure of a story shapes its pacing, emotional beats, and impact on the reader. Mastering story structure is not about following rigid formulas but about understanding the core principles that make stories resonate across cultures and generations.

At its heart, structure provides a foundation for your creativity, ensuring your story flows logically while leaving room for unexpected twists and emotional depth. Whether your tale is an epic fantasy, a gripping thriller, or an introspective drama, crafting a strong structure helps guide your readers through a meaningful and memorable experience.

In this chapter, we'll explore the fundamental principles of story structure and dive into advanced narrative models like the Three-Act Framework, The Hero's Journey, and others. Along the way, we'll examine how to adapt these models to suit your story's unique needs and discuss examples from iconic works to see these frameworks in action. By the end, you'll have the tools to shape a story that captures your creative vision while connecting deeply with your audience.

Let's begin with the basics of story structure: the Three-Act Framework.

The Basics of Story Structure: The Three-Act Framework
The Three-Act Framework is one of the most enduring and versatile storytelling structures. Its simplicity makes it an excellent foundation for writers at any stage, providing a clear roadmap while leaving room for creativity. At its core, the Three-Act Framework divides a story into three distinct phases: the beginning, middle, and end. Each phase serves a unique purpose in guiding the audience through the narrative while delivering emotional impact and resolution.

1. Act One: The Setup

The first act establishes the foundation of your story. It introduces the protagonist, the setting, and the central conflict or question that will drive the narrative. The key to a strong Act One is to draw readers into your world quickly, giving them a reason to care about the characters and their journey.

Essential Components:
- The Hook: Start with an event, question, or situation that grabs the reader's attention immediately.
  - Example: In The Hunger Games, Katniss volunteering as tribute within the first few chapters sets the stakes early.
- Establishing the Status Quo: Show the protagonist's "normal world" before their life is disrupted.
  - Example: Frodo's peaceful existence in the Shire in The Lord of the Rings helps contrast the later chaos.
- The Inciting Incident: This is the moment that propels the protagonist out of their comfort zone and into the story's central conflict.
  - Example: In Harry Potter and the Sorcerer's Stone, Harry's acceptance letter to Hogwarts is the event that changes everything.

Purpose: The setup must establish stakes, introduce key players, and spark curiosity, compelling readers to continue.

2. Act Two: The Confrontation

The second act is the longest and often the most challenging to write. Here, the protagonist encounters escalating challenges, meets allies and enemies, and begins to transform. This act deepens the story's themes and stakes while maintaining forward momentum.

Essential Components:
- Rising Action: A series of obstacles and conflicts that test the protagonist's resolve. These events must be increasingly challenging, keeping readers engaged.
  - Example: In The Matrix, Neo's training and encounters with agents steadily build tension.
- The Midpoint Twist: A significant event halfway through the story that shifts the stakes or reveals crucial information.
  - Example: In Star Wars: The Empire Strikes Back, Luke learns the shocking truth about his parentage.
- Character Growth: As the protagonist faces external challenges, they also undergo internal transformation.
  - Example: Elizabeth Bennet in Pride and Prejudice begins to see her own biases, prompting personal growth.

Purpose: This act focuses on conflict and development, pushing the protagonist closer to their breaking point while raising questions about how they'll overcome their challenges.

3. Act Three: The Resolution
The third act delivers the climax and resolves the story's central conflict. It's the moment of ultimate transformation for the protagonist, where they achieve—or fail to achieve—their goal. The resolution ties together loose threads and leaves the audience with a sense of closure.

Essential Components:
- The Climax: The story's peak moment of tension, where the protagonist confronts their greatest obstacle or antagonist.
    - Example: In The Lord of the Rings, Frodo and Sam's struggle to destroy the One Ring is the culmination of their journey.
- The Transformation: The protagonist emerges changed, having learned or achieved something significant.
    - Example: In The Great Gatsby, Nick Carraway reflects on Gatsby's tragic life and gains insight into his own values.
- Falling Action: After the climax, the story resolves remaining subplots, giving the audience closure.
    - Example: In The Hunger Games, Katniss and Peeta's return to District 12 provides a bittersweet sense of resolution.

Purpose: The resolution answers the story's central question and delivers an emotionally satisfying conclusion, whether triumphant or tragic.

Why the Three-Act Framework Works
- Universality: The Three-Act Framework mirrors the way people naturally experience stories, making it intuitive and accessible.
- Flexibility: While the structure provides a clear guide, it leaves room for creative interpretation and deviation.
- Emotional Rhythm: By following a rise-and-fall pattern of tension, the framework creates a rhythm that resonates with audiences.

The Three-Act Framework is a timeless and versatile tool for structuring your story. It helps ensure your narrative flows logically, builds emotional momentum, and delivers a satisfying conclusion. As you grow more confident, you can experiment with variations or incorporate elements from more advanced structures while maintaining the clarity and emotional power this framework provides.

Deepening Character Arcs in Novels

In novels, a well-crafted structure serves as the backbone of a story, providing the framework for profound character development and emotional depth. While novels afford the space to explore subtle character transformations, the key lies in choosing the narrative model that best amplifies your story's themes and intentions.

Advanced narrative structures—such as the Hero's Journey, the Puzzle Box, and others—allow writers to design arcs that are not only compelling but also resonate universally. These models offer a roadmap, but they are not restrictive blueprints. Instead, they empower writers to create immersive worlds and multidimensional characters, offering clarity while leaving room for creativity.

In this section, we'll explore the six most influential narrative models, each tailored to specific genres and storytelling goals. By understanding the strengths of these structures, you can align your narrative with reader expectations while crafting a story that is uniquely yours.

What Works Best? AI Insights on Genre and Structure

Storytelling thrives on structure, and the right framework can elevate a good story into something unforgettable. Different structures resonate with different types of narratives because they align with genre expectations, reader engagement patterns, and emotional rhythms. While some stories demand the sweeping arc of the Hero's Journey, others benefit from the layered intrigue of the Puzzle Box or the transformative focus of the Coming-of-Age structure.

The following section introduces six influential narrative models, each tailored to specific genres and storytelling goals. These structures aren't rigid rules—they're tools to help you shape your story's unique DNA. Whether you're drawn to one model that feels like the perfect fit for your current project or want to explore them all, this section is designed to inspire and guide.

If you're focused on completing your novel, feel free to concentrate on one structure that aligns with your vision and return to explore the others later. These models are here to provide clarity and direction, whether you're creating a tight, genre-specific tale or a narrative that defies convention. Let these frameworks serve as your creative allies, offering insights and techniques to bring your story to life.

The Six Core Narrative Structures

1. Adventure and Fantasy
The Hero's Journey For adventure or fantasy novels, one of the most time-tested structures is the Hero's Journey. This arc, first popularized by mythologist Joseph Campbell, follows a character as they leave their familiar world, face trials, grow stronger, and return transformed. This structure offers both an external adventure and an internal journey, ideal for genres that explore themes of bravery, loyalty, and self-discovery.

Example: The Hobbit by J.R.R. Tolkien takes readers through Bilbo Baggins' journey from an ordinary life in the Shire to a daring quest that transforms him into a hero. Each stage of the journey introduces new allies, challenges, and self-revelations, making it a rich narrative suited to the fantastical elements of Middle-earth.

2. Mystery and Thriller – The Puzzle Box Structure
Mystery and thriller genres often revolve around tension and revelation. These stories frequently utilize a Puzzle Box structure, where clues are gradually revealed, and each twist drives the reader closer to the resolution. In these narratives, characters uncover secrets in stages, with a carefully timed release of information to maintain suspense and engagement.

Example: In The Girl with the Dragon Tattoo by Stieg Larsson, each chapter unveils new details about the central mystery, keeping readers on edge as they follow both the investigation and the personal dynamics between the protagonists. This structure creates suspense by parceling out revelations that deepen both the mystery and the characters' relationships.

3. Romance – The Relationship-Driven Structure
In romance novels, readers expect a compelling emotional journey between characters, often driven by a combination of connection and conflict. The Emotional Arc commonly used in romance sees characters start with a form of tension or difference, overcome misunderstandings, and ultimately realize their love or bond. This structure is effective for romance because it emphasizes both internal and external obstacles that keep readers invested in the relationship's outcome.

Example: Pride and Prejudice by Jane Austen presents Elizabeth and Mr. Darcy as initially at odds due to misjudgments and societal pressures. Their emotional arc evolves as each character learns to see the other's true nature, with the structure of growing connection, tension, and ultimate realization creating a satisfying romantic payoff.

4. Horror – The Descent into Darkness
Horror novels typically follow a Descent into Darkness structure, where the main character or group encounters escalating threats that challenge their physical and psychological limits. This progression often leads to a climactic confrontation with the horror's source, leaving characters changed or haunted. Horror's appeal lies in the buildup of fear and tension, so pacing is crucial to guide readers through both dread and revelation.

Example: Stephen King's It builds fear through both external supernatural threats and the internal fears of each character. The "descent" often involves revisiting past traumas, uncovering unsettling truths, and eventually facing the monster, creating a blend of suspense and emotional resonance.

5. Science Fiction – The Exploration and Discovery Model
Science fiction often follows an Exploration and Discovery model, where characters navigate unknown worlds, futuristic technologies, or speculative scenarios. This structure allows room for philosophical questions and imaginative exploration, presenting a conflict that is often existential or societal, with the protagonist learning about their own humanity along the way.

Example: In Dune by Frank Herbert, Paul Atreides' journey on the desert planet of Arrakis leads to a deep exploration of power, ecology, and destiny. The narrative combines political intrigue with personal discovery, allowing readers to experience both the outer and inner landscapes of this expansive world.

6. Coming-of-Age Structure
Coming-of-age novels follow a growth structure, where the protagonist evolves from innocence to experience, often discovering their identity in the face of life's challenges. This arc is effective for stories centered on character growth and self-discovery, giving readers an intimate look at a young person's journey through pivotal moments.

Example: The Catcher in the Rye by J.D. Salinger follows Holden Caulfield as he navigates adolescence and grapples with complex feelings of alienation and belonging. This arc captures the rawness of growing up, making it universally relatable and impactful.

Finding the Right Structure for Your Story
While genre conventions offer a helpful starting point, don't feel restricted by them. Let these structures guide your story's pacing, tone, and emotional beats, but adapt them to suit the unique aspects of your characters and themes. As you write, remember that structure is a tool—use it to build the foundation for your story, but feel free to break or blend genres and structures as inspiration leads you.

Ultimately, these patterns emerged because they tap into universal themes, fears, and desires that resonate deeply with readers. Whether you're crafting an epic fantasy or an intimate romance, these tried-and-true frameworks can support you as you bring your vision to life.

The Six Core Narrative Structures: A Toolkit for Every Story
Storytelling, like human experience, is vast and diverse, yet certain structures consistently resonate with readers across genres, cultures, and time. These Six Core Narrative Structures, identified through AI analysis of countless successful works—ranging from ancient myths to contemporary bestsellers—serve as a guide to crafting stories that captivate and endure. By blending story structure, narrative frameworks, and character arcs, these models offer the tools you need to shape your story's DNA.

AI's analysis reveals that these structures act as flexible foundations rather than rigid formulas. They provide clarity and direction while leaving room for creativity, allowing you to craft narratives that align with your genre, themes, and storytelling goals. While each story often gravitates toward one dominant structure, most blend elements from multiple frameworks, creating layered and engaging storytelling experiences. These models are the key to balancing familiarity with innovation—ensuring your work feels both timeless and unique.

Think of these Six Core Narrative Structures as a toolkit designed to adapt to your needs. Each framework is built to support specific storytelling goals:
- Structure organizes the key beats and rhythm of your story.
- Framework determines how your story is delivered— chronologically, through flashbacks, or nested within layers.

- Character Arcs map the transformation of your characters, which often parallels and reinforces your chosen structure

The following sections will guide you through these six genre-specific storytelling models. For each, we'll examine:

- Why It Works: The appeal and emotional resonance of the structure.
- Key Elements: The stages or components that define the model.
- Examples in Action: How successful stories have used it to captivate readers.
- How to Apply It: Practical advice for tailoring the structure to your unique narrative.

Dive into the structure that aligns with your vision or explore all six for inspiration. This chapter provides insights not only into structure but also into how frameworks and character arcs naturally integrate into these models, allowing you to create stories that are both meaningful and unforgettable.

The Hero's Journey
The Hero's Journey is one of the most enduring and widely recognized narrative structures in storytelling. Rooted in Joseph Campbell's exploration of mythology and universal archetypes, it charts the journey of a central character as they grow, change, and overcome challenges. This structure resonates with readers because it mirrors the transformative experiences we all face, making it both relatable and inspiring.

Why It Works
The Hero's Journey resonates because it taps into a universal narrative pattern of transformation. At its heart, this structure reflects the human experience: venturing into the unknown, confronting fears, and emerging changed. It provides a framework that balances external action with internal growth, ensuring stories feel both dynamic and meaningful. Whether the hero triumphs, falters, or grows in unexpected ways, this structure provides the emotional depth and clarity that audiences crave.

Key Elements of the Hero's Journey
The Hero's Journey is built on specific stages that guide the story's progression. These stages provide clarity for the writer and a satisfying rhythm for the reader:

1. The Ordinary World: Introduces the hero's normal life, establishing their current reality and the stakes for change.
2. Call to Adventure: An event or challenge disrupts the hero's status quo and sets them on their path.
3. Refusal of the Call: The hero hesitates, revealing vulnerabilities or internal conflicts.
4. Meeting the Mentor: A guide appears to provide advice, tools, or inspiration.
5. Crossing the Threshold: The hero commits to the journey, leaving their ordinary world behind.
6. Tests, Allies, and Enemies: The hero faces obstacles and forms relationships that shape their growth.
7. The Ordeal: A major trial or crisis that forces the hero to confront their deepest fears.
8. Reward: The hero achieves a victory, gains knowledge, or finds clarity.
9. The Road Back and Resurrection: The hero faces a final challenge that tests their transformation.
10. Return with the Elixir: The hero returns to the ordinary world, changed by their journey.

Examples in Action
Some of the most beloved and successful stories have followed the Hero's Journey framework, demonstrating its versatility and enduring appeal:

- Frodo Baggins – The Lord of the Rings
    - Frodo's quiet life in the Shire is upended when he is tasked with destroying the One Ring. His journey through trials, alliances, and sacrifices transforms him into a character defined by resilience and wisdom.
- Harry Potter – Harry Potter and the Philosopher's Stone
    - Harry begins in the Ordinary World of the Dursleys' neglectful household before receiving his Call to Adventure with the invitation to Hogwarts. With the guidance of mentors like Dumbledore and Hagrid, he confronts his fears, defeats Voldemort's plans, and returns stronger and more self-assured.
- Katniss Everdeen – The Hunger Games
    - Katniss's Call to Adventure is her decision to volunteer for the Hunger Games. Through allies like Peeta and her own resourcefulness, she faces tests of survival, culminating in her symbolic rebellion against the Capitol.

How to Apply It

The Hero's Journey is a versatile structure that can be tailored to fit your story. Here's how to make the most of it:

- Anchor Your Protagonist in the Ordinary World: Begin by establishing your hero's normal life. Highlight their strengths, weaknesses, and what they stand to lose or gain from change.
  - Tip: Use this phase to build empathy for the hero and create a clear contrast with the adventure ahead.

- Create a Powerful Call to Adventure: Introduce an inciting incident that pushes the hero out of their comfort zone. Ensure it ties into the character's internal goals or fears.
  - Example: In The Matrix, Neo's Call to Adventure comes when Morpheus offers him the red pill, forcing him to decide whether to pursue the truth.

- Incorporate Memorable Mentors, Allies, and Enemies: Enrich the hero's journey with supporting characters who reflect or challenge their growth.
  - Tip: Mentors don't have to be infallible. Complex figures like Gandalf in The Lord of the Rings or Haymitch in The Hunger Games add depth by being both flawed and wise.

- Focus on Growth Through Conflict: The trials and tests your hero faces should force them to change. Make sure each challenge reveals something new about their character.
  - Example: In Mulan, each trial—from her training to her battle with the Huns—reinforces her journey of self-discovery and honor.

- Deliver a Meaningful Transformation: The hero's return to the ordinary world should reflect their internal growth. Whether they succeed, fail, or achieve a bittersweet victory, the transformation should feel earned and impactful.
  - Tip: Ensure the final resolution ties back to the story's opening, showing how far the hero has come.

Conclusion: Crafting Memorable Arcs with the Hero's Journey

The Hero's Journey remains one of the most adaptable and emotionally resonant storytelling structures, offering a balance of external adventure and internal transformation. Its stages provide a clear guide for writers while leaving room for creativity and personal interpretation. By aligning your protagonist's journey with this framework, you can craft a narrative that feels both timeless and deeply personal.

The Puzzle Box Structure
The Puzzle Box Structure is a captivating narrative model that
thrives on mystery, gradual revelation, and intellectual engagement.
Popular in mystery, thriller, and literary fiction, it presents the
story as a series of interwoven puzzles or enigmas. Readers are
drawn into a dance of suspense, piecing together clues alongside—
or ahead of—the characters.

This structure isn't just about solving a mystery; it's about engaging
readers on a cerebral and emotional level. By withholding key
pieces of the narrative and strategically revealing them, Puzzle Box
stories create an active reading experience. They challenge the
audience to think critically, anticipate twists, and reassess previous
events in light of new information. As such, this framework is
perfect for writers aiming to craft multilayered and immersive
narratives.

Why It Works
The Puzzle Box Structure resonates with readers because it
leverages suspense, curiosity, and gradual revelation. It rewards
engagement and stimulates intellectual satisfaction by inviting
readers to participate in solving the story's central mystery. This
narrative model works especially well when coupled with dynamic
characters, red herrings, and layered storytelling techniques.

AI analysis highlights why the Puzzle Box Structure excels:
1. Engagement Through Mystery: By posing intriguing questions
   early, this structure hooks readers and keeps them invested as
   they seek answers.
2. Satisfying Complexity: Gradual revelations allow the story to
   build organically, creating a tapestry of interconnected clues
   that leads to a rewarding conclusion.
3. Intellectual Challenge: Readers enjoy the active role of
   decoding layered narratives, particularly when twists
   recontextualize earlier events.

Key Elements of the Puzzle Box Structure
The Puzzle Box Structure comprises specific elements designed to
captivate and sustain reader interest. Here's how to build your
narrative step-by-step:

1. The Hook: An Intriguing Question or Enigmatic Event
A Puzzle Box story begins with an attention-grabbing moment.
This could be a mysterious event, an enigmatic character, or a
provocative question that sets the stage for the story's central
puzzle.

- AI Insight: Opening with ambiguity or an unresolved conflict compels readers to engage immediately, seeking answers.
- Example: In Gone Girl by Gillian Flynn, Amy Dunne's disappearance poses a central mystery that unfolds in unexpected ways.

2. Fragmented Revelations: Slowly Unfolding Clues
Information in Puzzle Box narratives is rarely presented in a linear fashion. Instead, details are scattered across the plot, creating layers that readers must piece together.
- AI Insight: Fragmented storytelling keeps readers active and immersed, appealing to those who enjoy intellectual engagement.
- Example: In The Girl on the Train by Paula Hawkins, shifting perspectives and timelines reveal critical details in a non-linear manner, gradually reshaping the narrative.

3. Red Herrings: Adding Layers of Suspense and Misdirection
Red herrings—false clues or misleading information—heighten suspense and keep readers guessing.
- AI Insight: Successful red herrings maintain credibility while deflecting attention from the true answer, ensuring a satisfying twist.
- Example: In The Da Vinci Code by Dan Brown, false leads challenge both the protagonist and the reader, building anticipation for the final reveal.

4. Dual or Multiple Perspectives: Different Angles on the Same Puzzle
Introducing multiple perspectives allows readers to see various facets of the mystery, deepening their engagement.
- AI Insight: Alternating viewpoints sustain tension by revealing only fragments of the bigger picture.
- Example: Big Little Lies by Liane Moriarty uses alternating perspectives to uncover how seemingly disconnected events intertwine.

5. Flashbacks and Non-Linear Timelines: Context Through Disjointed Pieces
Flashbacks and non-linear timelines enrich Puzzle Box stories by offering context while preserving mystery.
- AI Insight: Flashbacks strategically placed at critical junctures deepen emotional resonance and enhance the mystery.
- Example: Rebecca by Daphne du Maurier uses flashbacks to unveil layers of intrigue surrounding the titular character's past.

6. Hidden Motives and Unreliable Narrators: Layering Complexity
Unreliable narrators or characters with concealed motives add
depth and uncertainty to the narrative.

- AI Insight: By challenging readers to discern truth from
  deception, this element fosters cognitive engagement and adds
  narrative richness.
- Example: The Secret History by Donna Tartt features a
  narrator whose subjective recounting invites readers to infer
  hidden truths.

Bringing It All Together: The Final Reveal
The climax of a Puzzle Box narrative delivers the final pieces of the
puzzle, recontextualizing the story and providing a satisfying
payoff.

- AI Insight: Effective reveals balance predictability with
  surprise, rewarding readers for their engagement while leaving
  room for reflection.
- Example: And Then There Were None by Agatha Christie ties
  every clue into a coherent, shocking resolution that redefines
  the story.

How to Apply It
To craft your Puzzle Box story:

- Start with a Compelling Mystery: Introduce an intriguing
  enigma early.
- Layer Your Clues Strategically: Use fragmented revelations to
  maintain tension.
- Deploy Red Herrings and Unreliable Narrators: Keep readers
  guessing.
- Build Toward a Satisfying Reveal: Ensure the resolution ties
  every element together.

Conclusion: Crafting an Engaging Puzzle Box
The Puzzle Box Structure invites readers into a dynamic
storytelling experience, blending suspense, intellect, and emotional
depth. With AI's insights, you can refine your narrative, ensuring
every twist, clue, and revelation resonates with readers. This
structure isn't just about solving a puzzle—it's about creating an
unforgettable journey that keeps readers invested from the first
question to the final reveal.

The Relationship-Driven Structure
Relationships are the backbone of countless powerful stories. The Relationship-Driven Structure places these connections—whether romantic, platonic, familial, or adversarial—at the heart of the narrative. Instead of centering on external events or mysteries, the story's emotional momentum arises from the growth, tension, and transformation within relationships. This structure thrives in genres like drama, romance, and character-driven fiction, where the push and pull between characters forms the core of the narrative.

Unlike structures that focus on external plot progression, the Relationship-Driven Structure relies on emotional beats: moments of connection, conflict, and resolution. These emotional arcs define the story's rhythm and depth, providing a framework that mirrors the complexity of real-life relationships.

Why It Works
The Relationship-Driven Structure resonates because it focuses on what readers find most relatable: the highs and lows of human connection. Whether it's the tension of a love-hate relationship, the fragility of a strained friendship, or the bittersweet nature of loss, these dynamics evoke powerful emotions and keep readers invested.

AI analysis highlights why this structure excels:
1. Universal Relatability: Everyone has experienced relationships in some form, making these stories accessible across cultures and genres.
2. Emotional Investment: Readers are drawn to characters whose relationships mirror their own hopes, fears, and struggles.
3. Narrative Momentum: Connection and conflict provide natural turning points, keeping the story engaging even in the absence of high-stakes external events.

Key Stages of the Relationship-Driven Structure
This structure unfolds through stages that mirror the evolution of relationships. These beats provide a roadmap for crafting compelling emotional arcs.

1. The Initial Bond: Establishing the Connection
The story begins with the formation of a significant relationship. This could be the start of a romance, the rekindling of an estranged friendship, or the foundation of an uneasy alliance.
- AI Insight: Readers connect to characters through small but meaningful gestures or shared experiences, even if the relationship starts with tension or opposition.

- Examples:
  - Pride and Prejudice by Jane Austen: Elizabeth and Darcy's relationship begins with mutual disdain, setting the stage for gradual change.
  - The Hunger Games by Suzanne Collins: Katniss and Rue's bond forms over shared vulnerability, instantly endearing them to readers.

Takeaway: Establish a connection that feels real and layered, whether through camaraderie, tension, or shared goals.

2. Growth Through Shared Moments

The relationship deepens as characters share experiences that reveal vulnerabilities or mutual understanding. These moments create trust, intimacy, and emotional stakes.

- AI Insight: Vulnerability is key. When characters open up, readers are drawn into their world.
- Examples:
  - The Road by Cormac McCarthy: The father and son's journey is punctuated by tender, protective moments that strengthen their bond.
  - Jane Eyre by Charlotte Brontë: Jane and Mr. Rochester's shared secrets and honesty create a connection that defies societal norms.

Takeaway: Build relationships through small but powerful moments that reveal inner truths and deepen emotional ties.

3. Rising Conflict: Testing the Relationship

Tension enters the relationship, challenging its strength. This could come from internal conflicts (misunderstandings or clashing values) or external pressures (society, family, or survival).

- AI Insight: Conflict drives character growth and narrative momentum, forcing characters to confront their flaws or differences.
- Examples:
  - The Great Gatsby by F. Scott Fitzgerald: Gatsby's idealism collides with Daisy's pragmatism, creating emotional friction that drives the story.
  - Breaking Bad: Walter White and Jesse Pinkman's manipulative yet co-dependent partnership is filled with power struggles and betrayals.

Takeaway: Ensure conflicts are deeply personal, arising from the characters' motivations and fears.

4. The Breaking Point: Crisis in the Relationship

The relationship reaches a climax where its survival is at stake. This moment often forces characters to make difficult choices, revealing their true priorities.

- AI Insight: The breaking point should feel inevitable, a culmination of the relationship's dynamics and conflicts.
- Examples:
  o Wuthering Heights by Emily Brontë: Heathcliff and Catherine's toxic bond culminates in emotional devastation.
  o The Kite Runner by Khaled Hosseini: Amir's betrayal of Hassan creates a rift that drives the story's emotional core.

Takeaway: Make the breaking point emotionally resonant, showing how it shapes or reshapes the characters' connections.

5. Resolution: Reconciliation or Separation

The relationship reaches a resolution, whether through healing, transformation, or finality. This stage reflects the journey's impact on the characters and the broader story.

- AI Insight: Resolutions resonate when they feel earned, aligning with the characters' growth and choices.
- Examples:
  o To Kill a Mockingbird by Harper Lee: Scout's evolving understanding of Boo Radley resolves with a heartfelt moment of connection.
  o Anna Karenina by Leo Tolstoy: Anna's tragic end reflects the culmination of her strained relationships and inner conflict.

Takeaway: End the arc in a way that feels authentic to the characters' journeys, leaving readers satisfied or contemplative.

How to Apply It

- Choose Your Central Relationship: Decide which connection will drive your story—romantic, familial, platonic, or adversarial.
- Focus on Emotional Beats: Plan moments of connection, tension, and resolution that reflect the arc of the relationship.
- Balance Internal and External Forces: Ensure the relationship is shaped by both personal dynamics and external pressures.
- Use Subtext and Body Language: Deepen emotional resonance with gestures, silences, and unspoken cues.

Examples of Relationship-Driven Stories
- Romance:
  - Me Before You by Jojo Moyes: The bond between Louisa and Will transforms both characters emotionally, despite their differences and challenges.
- Friendship:
  - Of Mice and Men by John Steinbeck: George and Lennie's friendship is both their strength and their ultimate tragedy.
- Rivalry:
  - Sherlock Holmes and Moriarty: Their adversarial dynamic drives the tension and intellectual engagement of Arthur Conan Doyle's stories.

Conclusion: Crafting Meaningful Connections
The Relationship-Driven Structure offers a versatile framework for stories centered on emotional depth and interpersonal dynamics. By focusing on connection, tension, and resolution, you can craft narratives that resonate deeply with readers, mirroring the complexity of human relationships.

With AI insights, you can refine these relationships, ensuring each interaction is authentic and impactful. Whether your story ends in reconciliation, transformation, or separation, the journey of these connections will leave a lasting impression on your audience.

The Descent into Darkness
The Descent into Darkness is a compelling narrative structure centered on a character's journey into their most profound fears, weaknesses, or moral dilemmas. This structure captivates readers by exploring the duality of light and shadow within human nature. By immersing a character in intense inner conflict and external challenges, this arc reveals their capacity for resilience, vulnerability, or ultimate surrender.

Why It Works
The Descent into Darkness appeals to readers on a primal level. It mirrors the human experience of confronting fears, weaknesses, and the choices that define us. Whether the story ends in redemption or tragedy, this structure resonates because:
1. Emotional Depth: Readers are drawn to characters who reveal their flaws and struggle against them.
2. Psychological Tension: Inner battles heighten engagement, creating empathy even for morally ambiguous characters.
3. Universal Themes: This structure explores timeless questions about morality, identity, and survival.

Key Stages of the Descent into Darkness
A.I. has analyzed this structure and identified six essential stages. These stages build upon one another, guiding readers through the character's gradual fall or transformation.

1. The Catalyst: Setting the Descent in Motion
The story begins with a catalyst—a moment that forces the protagonist to confront their darker impulses or vulnerabilities. This event sets the emotional stakes and foreshadows the descent.
- A.I. Insight: The catalyst should feel personal, making the descent feel unavoidable and deeply tied to the character's psyche.
- Example: In Macbeth by William Shakespeare, the witches' prophecy awakens Macbeth's ambition, setting him on a destructive path.

2. Crossing the Threshold: A Point of No Return
The character makes an irreversible choice, committing to their dark journey. This decision often involves betrayal, moral compromise, or a significant turning point.
- A.I. Insight: A strong threshold moment creates narrative momentum, making the descent feel inevitable.
- Example: In Breaking Bad, Walter White's decision to continue manufacturing meth solidifies his transformation from a well-meaning father to a morally ambiguous antihero.

3. Isolation and Alienation: Losing Support and Connection

The descent isolates the character from their support systems, whether through self-imposed exile or external circumstances.

- A.I. Insight: Isolation deepens empathy, as readers witness the character's struggle without distractions.
- Example: In The Picture of Dorian Gray by Oscar Wilde, Dorian's descent into excess and moral decay leaves him estranged from genuine connections.

4. The Encounter with Inner Demons: Facing the Self

At this stage, the character confronts their fears, guilt, or moral weaknesses directly. These encounters are often psychological, blending internal and external struggles.

- A.I. Insight: Readers are captivated by vivid depictions of internal conflict, allowing them to witness the character's unfiltered thoughts and fears.
- Example: In Heart of Darkness by Joseph Conrad, Marlow's journey to meet Kurtz becomes an exploration of humanity's darkest instincts.

5. The Revelation or Epiphany: Understanding the Darkness

The climax of the descent brings a revelation. The character gains insight into their actions or uncovers a hard truth about themselves.

- A.I. Insight: Impactful revelations add emotional weight, showing the character's complexity.
- Example: In Crime and Punishment by Fyodor Dostoevsky, Raskolnikov realizes the moral consequences of his crime, leading to a transformative confession.

6. The Final Choice: Redemption or Ruin

The journey ends with a defining choice: will the character seek redemption or fully embrace the darkness?

- A.I. Insight: This decision should feel earned, reflecting the character's arc and leaving a lasting impression.
- Example: In The Strange Case of Dr. Jekyll and Mr. Hyde by Robert Louis Stevenson, Dr. Jekyll's inability to resist his darker impulses leads to his tragic transformation into Mr. Hyde.

How to Apply It
- Personalize the Descent: Tie the character's struggles to their core fears, desires, or beliefs.
- Layer the Conflict: Alternate between external challenges and internal battles to maintain tension.
- Plan the Revelation: Ensure the climax reveals something meaningful about the character, offering emotional payoff.

- Earn the Resolution: Make the final choice consistent with the character's journey, whether it leads to redemption or ruin.

Examples of Stories with Descent into Darkness
- Tragedy: Othello by William Shakespeare explores jealousy and manipulation, leading to devastating consequences.
- Thriller: Shutter Island by Dennis Lehane features a protagonist grappling with unraveling reality, blending psychological tension with mystery.
- Fantasy: The Lord of the Rings by J.R.R. Tolkien shows Frodo tempted by the Ring's power, highlighting the moral cost of heroism.

Conclusion: Crafting a Compelling Descent
The Descent into Darkness invites readers into the depths of human nature, exploring the choices that define us. By carefully crafting each stage—from the catalyst to the final choice—writers can create narratives that linger in readers' minds. With A.I. insights guiding you, this structure becomes a powerful tool for storytelling, offering profound emotional depth and timeless resonance.

The Exploration and Discovery Model
The Exploration and Discovery Model emphasizes the thrill of
uncovering the unknown. Whether it's venturing into uncharted
lands, delving into the depths of human consciousness, or exploring
revolutionary ideas, this narrative structure captivates by
immersing readers in the process of discovery. This structure is
especially effective in genres like adventure, fantasy, science fiction,
and literary fiction, where the narrative revolves around the
protagonist's journey through unfamiliar territories or concepts.

Why It Works
This structure resonates with readers because it mirrors the human
experience of curiosity, learning, and growth. The act of discovery
fuels the story's progression, making readers feel as though they're
embarking on the journey alongside the protagonist. Key reasons
for its effectiveness include:
- Curiosity and Suspense: Readers are drawn in by the promise
  of uncovering secrets and truths.
- Immersive World-Building: Detailed settings and intricate plots
  ground readers in the narrative.
- Character Growth: Discovery isn't just external; it transforms
  the protagonist, offering emotional and intellectual depth.

Key Stages of the Exploration and Discovery Model
Drawing from AI's insights and timeless storytelling practices, the
following stages guide writers in creating an engaging narrative of
exploration:

1. The Call to Adventure: Inviting Curiosity
The story begins with a catalyst—a map, a mysterious event, or a
sudden question that beckons the protagonist into the unknown.
- A.I. Insight: A strong call to adventure hooks readers
  immediately, providing intrigue while hinting at the narrative's
  potential.
- Example: In Alice's Adventures in Wonderland by Lewis
  Carroll, Alice's curiosity about the White Rabbit leads her into
  a fantastical world.

2. Entering the Unknown: First Encounters and New Realities
The protagonist steps into the unfamiliar, encountering strange
sights, new rules, or unexpected challenges. This stage immerses
readers in the story's world.
- A.I. Insight: Vivid descriptions of first encounters help establish
  the story's setting and tone.
- Example: In The Golden Compass by Philip Pullman, Lyra's
  introduction to a world of armored bears and daemons
  expands the narrative's scope.

3. The Learning Curve: Gathering Knowledge and Making Mistakes

The protagonist begins to understand the new environment, often through trial and error. Mistakes and discoveries deepen engagement, showing the stakes and complexity of the world.

- A.I. Insight: This stage builds empathy and investment as readers experience the protagonist's growth alongside them.
- Example: In The Name of the Wind by Patrick Rothfuss, Kvothe navigates the complexities of magic and alchemy, revealing the world's depth.

4. Discovery of Secrets: Uncovering Hidden Truths

At this stage, the protagonist begins to unravel the story's mysteries, challenging their initial perceptions.

- A.I. Insight: Readers are captivated by unexpected twists and revelations, especially those that subvert expectations.
- Example: In The Shadow of the Wind by Carlos Ruiz Zafón, Daniel unravels the secrets surrounding a mysterious book, pulling readers deeper into the narrative.

5. Facing Challenges: Obstacles to Understanding

Challenges intensify as the protagonist encounters physical, emotional, or intellectual hurdles that test their resolve.

- A.I. Insight: These obstacles increase tension, making victories feel hard-won and meaningful.
- Example: In Life of Pi by Yann Martel, Pi's struggle for survival on a lifeboat with a tiger showcases both external and internal challenges.

6. The Moment of Wonder: Experiencing Awe and Transformation

A pivotal moment of awe or enlightenment marks the narrative's high point. The protagonist's perceptions of the world—or themselves—are irrevocably altered.

- A.I. Insight: Transformative moments offer emotional payoff, creating a sense of wonder and connection.
- Example: In The Alchemist by Paulo Coelho, Santiago's realization about the interconnectedness of all things epitomizes the journey's spiritual and transformative essence.

7. Revelation and Return: Integrating New Knowledge

The protagonist returns to their familiar world, changed by their discoveries. This resolution reflects their growth and brings closure.

- A.I. Insight: Readers value a satisfying conclusion where the protagonist's transformation is evident.
- Example: In Journey to the Center of the Earth by Jules Verne, the protagonists emerge from their subterranean voyage profoundly changed.

How to Apply It
- Establish Stakes Early: Make the call to adventure compelling and personal to the protagonist.
- Balance World-Building with Action: Avoid overwhelming readers with details; integrate them organically through the protagonist's journey.
- Create Layers of Discovery: Let each revelation add complexity, challenging both the protagonist and readers.
- Focus on Growth: Ensure the protagonist's transformation feels authentic, tied to their experiences throughout the story.

Examples of Stories Using the Exploration and Discovery Model
- Adventure: Treasure Island by Robert Louis Stevenson uses exploration to fuel both plot and character development.
- Science Fiction: Dune by Frank Herbert combines external discovery with internal transformation, exploring themes of power and destiny.
- Fantasy: The Hobbit by J.R.R. Tolkien intertwines world-building with Bilbo's growth from a reluctant adventurer to a hero.

Conclusion: Crafting an Engaging Exploration and Discovery Arc
The Exploration and Discovery Model invites readers to join the protagonist on a journey of awe and transformation. By integrating vivid settings, layered mysteries, and authentic character growth, writers can craft stories that resonate deeply. With AI insights guiding each stage, this structure becomes a tool for creating immersive narratives that celebrate the thrill of the unknown.

The Coming-of-Age Structure

The Coming-of-Age Structure centers on the transformative journey from innocence to maturity, capturing the universal experience of self-discovery and personal growth. This structure isn't just about growing up—it's about confronting challenges, making choices, and emerging with a deeper understanding of oneself and the world. From literary classics to contemporary tales, the Coming-of-Age Structure continues to resonate because it reflects the struggles and triumphs of finding one's place in the world.

Why It Works

The Coming-of-Age Structure appeals to readers because it mirrors their own journeys of growth and self-discovery. This narrative model works especially well for exploring themes of identity, relationships, and the transition from childhood to adulthood.

AI analysis highlights the enduring appeal of this structure:
1. Relatability: Readers connect with protagonists whose struggles reflect their own or evoke empathy.
2. Emotional Investment: The gradual transformation of the protagonist provides a satisfying narrative arc.
3. Timelessness: Themes of self-discovery and growth resonate across cultures and generations.

Key Stages of the Coming-of-Age Structure

The Coming-of-Age Structure unfolds through distinct stages that mirror the process of personal growth and self-realization. Each stage offers opportunities for character development and emotional resonance.

1. The Ordinary World: Establishing Innocence

The story begins in the protagonist's familiar world, highlighting their naivety, innocence, or inexperience. This baseline helps contrast their eventual transformation.
- AI Insight: Establish a relatable starting point that reflects the protagonist's initial limitations or misconceptions.
- Example: In To Kill a Mockingbird by Harper Lee, Scout Finch's childhood perspective frames her initial innocence about the racial injustices in her town.

2. The Call to Change: A Catalyst for Growth

A significant event disrupts the protagonist's status quo, forcing them to confront new realities or challenges. This call often introduces the central conflict or theme of the story.
- AI Insight: The catalyst should feel personal, creating stakes that drive the protagonist's transformation.

- Example: In Harry Potter and the Philosopher's Stone, Harry's invitation to Hogwarts begins his journey of self-discovery and belonging.

3. Early Trials: Testing the Protagonist

As the protagonist steps into an unfamiliar world or situation, they encounter obstacles that challenge their beliefs, values, or abilities. These early trials shape their initial growth and set the tone for their journey.

- AI Insight: Early trials should reflect the protagonist's internal struggles while advancing the plot.
- Example: In The Catcher in the Rye by J.D. Salinger, Holden Caulfield's encounters in New York City test his cynicism and search for authenticity.

4. Mentorship and Guidance: Finding Support

A mentor or guide often appears to help the protagonist navigate their journey. This figure may provide wisdom, encouragement, or serve as a cautionary example.

- AI Insight: Mentors can embody the protagonist's potential future, offering insight into their choices and consequences.
- Example: In The Perks of Being a Wallflower by Stephen Chbosky, Charlie's friendships with Sam and Patrick help him explore his identity and emotions.

5. The Crisis of Identity: Confronting the Self

The protagonist faces a pivotal challenge that forces them to question their values, identity, or place in the world. This moment often represents the emotional or thematic climax of the story.

- AI Insight: This crisis should feel deeply personal, reflecting the protagonist's internal and external struggles.
- Example: In Jane Eyre by Charlotte Brontë, Jane's refusal to compromise her principles when offered wealth and marriage reflects her growth and self-respect.

6. Transformation: Emerging Stronger

After confronting their fears or overcoming challenges, the protagonist undergoes a transformation. They gain clarity, strength, or maturity, often realizing their true potential or values.

- AI Insight: Ensure the transformation feels earned, tied to the protagonist's choices and experiences.
- Example: In The Kite Runner by Khaled Hosseini, Amir's decision to rescue Sohrab represents his redemption and emotional maturity.

7. Return to the Ordinary World: A Changed Perspective
The story concludes with the protagonist returning to their familiar world or a new one, carrying the lessons and growth they've achieved. This resolution ties together the narrative's themes and the protagonist's arc.
- AI Insight: The resolution should reflect the protagonist's transformation while leaving room for reflection.
- Example: In The Lord of the Flies by William Golding, Ralph's rescue brings him back to civilization, but he is forever changed by his harrowing experiences.

How to Apply It
- Choose a Relatable Catalyst: Make the event or challenge that sparks growth personal and meaningful.
- Focus on Emotional Beats: Highlight the protagonist's internal struggles and emotional journey.
- Develop Layered Mentors: Include figures who challenge, guide, or reflect the protagonist's potential.
- Earn the Transformation: Ensure the protagonist's growth feels authentic, tied to the story's events and themes.

Examples of Stories Using the Coming-of-Age Structure
- Classic Literature: Great Expectations by Charles Dickens follows Pip's journey from naivety to self-awareness.
- Contemporary Fiction: The Hate U Give by Angie Thomas explores Starr's growth as she confronts systemic racism and her own identity.
- Fantasy: Eragon by Christopher Paolini intertwines the protagonist's personal growth with his journey as a Dragon Rider.

Conclusion: Crafting Stories of Growth and Transformation
The Coming-of-Age Structure is a timeless narrative model that reflects the universal journey of self-discovery. By guiding your protagonist through challenges, crises, and transformations, you can create stories that resonate deeply with readers. With AI insights, you can refine each stage, ensuring your narrative captures the complexity and beauty of personal growth.

The Six Core Narrative Structures

In this section, we've explored six narrative structures that serve as powerful tools for shaping your story. Each structure offers a unique framework, catering to specific genres, themes, and storytelling goals. While each model is distinct, they share common elements that can be combined or adapted to create layered and dynamic narratives.

1. **Three-Act Framework:** The Foundation of Storytelling
   - Key Strength: A simple yet effective structure that divides a story into Setup, Confrontation, and Resolution.
   - Use For: Stories that benefit from clear progression and pacing.
   - What It Offers: A solid backbone for most genres, ensuring the story hits key beats in a satisfying rhythm.

2. **The Hero's Journey:** Transformation Through Trials
   - Key Strength: Universally recognized, focusing on a protagonist's growth through challenges.
   - Use For: Adventure, fantasy, and epic tales with a focus on internal and external transformation.
   - What It Offers: A step-by-step guide to creating a story of personal growth and heroism.

3. **Puzzle Box Structure:** Layered Mystery and Revelation
   - Key Strength: Keeps readers guessing by withholding key information and revealing it gradually.
   - Use For: Mysteries, thrillers, and literary fiction with intricate plots.
   - What It Offers: Tools to build suspense and deliver satisfying twists and revelations.

4. **Relationship-Driven Structure:** Emotional Connection and Conflict
   - Key Strength: Focuses on the push-and-pull dynamics of relationships as the core of the narrative.
   - Use For: Dramas, romances, and stories emphasizing character interaction.
   - What It Offers: A framework for exploring meaningful connections and emotional depth.

5. **Descent into Darkness:** The Shadowed Path
   - Key Strength: Explores moral dilemmas, psychological tension, and transformation through adversity.
   - Use For: Tragedies, psychological thrillers, and antihero narratives.
   - What It Offers: A guide to creating compelling, emotionally complex stories of decline or redemption.

6. Exploration and Discovery: The Thrill of the Unknown
- Key Strength: Centers on the wonder and transformation that come from uncovering new worlds, ideas, or truths.
- Use For: Adventure, fantasy, science fiction, and philosophical narratives.
- What It Offers: A method for crafting immersive stories that highlight curiosity, growth, and wonder.

Conclusion: Interconnections and Complementary Approaches
While each structure is presented as distinct, they are not mutually exclusive. Many successful stories blend elements of multiple structures to create rich, multidimensional narratives. For instance:

- The Hero's Journey often incorporates Relationship-Driven elements, as allies and mentors shape the hero's growth.
- The Puzzle Box Structure can intertwine with Descent into Darkness, as uncovering mysteries may parallel the protagonist's internal unraveling.
- Coming-of-Age stories frequently overlap with Exploration and Discovery, as characters grow through their encounters with new environments or ideas.

Using These Structures Together
Think of these structures as tools in a writer's kit:
- Choose one as your primary framework, ensuring it aligns with your story's goals.
- Borrow elements from others to add depth, complexity, or emotional resonance.
- Allow your creativity to guide the way, using these models as flexible guides rather than rigid templates.

With these six structures at your disposal, you're equipped to craft stories that resonate deeply with readers, offering clarity in structure while leaving room for innovation and personal expression. Now, it's time to choose your path and bring your narrative vision to life. The possibilities are limitless!

Chapter 10: Writing Beginnings That Hook Readers

The beginning of your story is your first chance to capture a reader's attention. Whether it's the opening line, the stakes you establish, or the intrigue you create, every word in your opening matters. This chapter explores how to craft an irresistible start to your novel, breaking it down into three key elements: a killer first line, establishing stakes, and balancing intrigue with clarity.

Crafting a Killer First Line
Your first line is the doorway to your story. It sets the tone, sparks curiosity, and invites readers to step into your world. A well-crafted opening line can make the difference between a reader turning the page or putting the book down.

What Makes a Great First Line?
- Emotionally Charged: A first line that evokes curiosity, humor, or suspense immediately draws readers in.
- Hints at Conflict: Introduce tension or a problem right from the start.
- Unique Voice: Establish the tone and personality of your narrative early.

Examples of Iconic First Lines
- "It was a bright cold day in April, and the clocks were striking thirteen." – 1984 by George Orwell
  - Why It Works: The surreal image immediately creates unease, setting the tone for a dystopian world.
- "Call me Ishmael." – Moby-Dick by Herman Melville
  - Why It Works: This line's simplicity and intrigue draw readers into a narrator with a mysterious past.
- "Mr. and Mrs. Dursley, of number four, Privet Drive, were proud to say that they were perfectly normal, thank you very much." – Harry Potter and the Philosopher's Stone by J.K. Rowling
  - Why It Works: This opening establishes tone, humor, and hints at the extraordinary within the ordinary.
- "There was a boy called Eustace Clarence Scrubb, and he almost deserved it." – The Voyage of the Dawn Treader by C.S. Lewis
  - Why It Works: The humor and subtle judgment about Eustace invite curiosity about his character.
- "Mother died today." – The Stranger by Albert Camus
  - Why It Works: This stark, emotionless statement immediately raises questions about the narrator's detachment and the circumstances.

- "It was a pleasure to burn." – Fahrenheit 451 by Ray Bradbury
  - Why It Works: This opening shocks the reader with its reversal of expectations, setting the tone for a dystopian world.

AI Insights on Crafting First Lines
- AI tools can analyze opening lines to ensure they evoke strong emotional reactions or align with popular trends in your genre.
- Experiment by generating multiple versions of your first line and test their impact on beta readers or writing groups.

Takeaway: Start with a line that leaves no doubt about the mood, voice, or stakes of your story. It doesn't need to explain everything —it just needs to make readers curious.

Establishing Stakes Quickly
The first few pages of your story should give readers a reason to care. By establishing what's at stake early, you ensure your audience is emotionally invested in the outcome.

- What Are Stakes?
  - Stakes answer the question, "Why should the reader care?" They could be personal (a character's survival), relational (a friendship at risk), or global (saving the world).
- Techniques to Establish Stakes
  - Introduce Conflict Immediately: Start with a problem or tension that hints at larger issues.
    - Example: "The man in black fled across the desert, and the gunslinger followed." – The Gunslinger by Stephen King. This line instantly sets up a chase, creating urgency.
  - Show What the Character Has to Lose: Highlight the character's stakes through their emotions or decisions.
    - Example: In The Hunger Games, Katniss's choice to volunteer for her sister immediately shows her love and the dangers she faces.
  - Pose a Question: Create stakes by introducing a mystery or unanswered question.
    - Example: In Rebecca by Daphne du Maurier, the opening line, "Last night I dreamt I went to Manderley again," sets up a haunting enigma.
- AI Insights on Stakes
  - AI can help identify whether your opening effectively sets stakes by analyzing the urgency and emotional engagement of your first chapter.

Takeaway: Stakes don't have to be grand, but they must be clear. Readers should know what's at risk and why it matters.

Balancing Intrigue with Clarity

A strong beginning strikes a balance between creating curiosity and providing enough context for readers to understand what's happening. If it's too vague, readers may feel lost; if it's too detailed, the mystery is lost.

- The Role of Intrigue
  - Intrigue invites readers to ask questions and imagine possibilities. It teases rather than explains, drawing them deeper into the story.
- Avoiding Overload
  - What to Avoid:
    - Excessive Backstory: Save detailed history for later; focus on immediate action or emotion.
    - Overcomplicated Descriptions: Don't overwhelm readers with too much world-building in the opening.
  - What to Aim For:
    - Provide enough detail to ground the reader without overloading them.
- Examples of Intrigue and Clarity
  - "The morning burned so August-hot, the marsh's moist breath hung the oaks and pines with fog." – Where the Crawdads Sing by Delia Owens
    - Why It Works:
      - Atmosphere: The vivid imagery immediately immerses the reader in the setting, making the marsh a character in itself.
      - Tone: The sensory details convey an intimate, almost nostalgic connection to the land, setting up the novel's themes of survival and isolation.
      - Intrigue: The vivid description raises questions about the role the marsh plays in the story and who inhabits this world.
  - "When the lights went off, the accompanist kissed her." – Bel Canto by Ann Patchett
    - Why It Works: This opening is both surprising and evocative, immediately pulling the reader into a moment of intimacy and mystery.

AI Insights on Clarity
- Use AI tools to check the readability and flow of your opening paragraphs. These tools can highlight unclear phrasing or overly complex sentences.

Takeaway: Intrigue keeps readers engaged, but clarity ensures they stay on track. A strong opening provides just enough information to hook readers while leaving them eager to learn more.

Conclusion: Mastering the Art of Beginnings
Your opening is your chance to make a lasting first impression. A killer first line, clear stakes, and a balance of intrigue and clarity will ensure readers keep turning the pages. With AI insights and examples from literary masters, you can refine your beginning to capture the hearts and minds of your audience. Now, it's time to craft an opening that demands attention—your story deserves nothing less.

Chapter 11: Building Conflict and Stakes

Conflict and stakes are the engines that drive your story forward. They create tension, reveal character depth, and keep readers emotionally invested. In this chapter, we'll explore the types of conflict that make stories compelling, how to escalate stakes naturally, and how to craft high-stakes storytelling that leaves a lasting impact.

Types of Conflict: Internal, External, and Relational
Conflict is the heart of storytelling, and understanding its different forms helps you create dynamic and layered narratives. Most conflicts can be categorized into three types:
1. Internal Conflict
- Definition: A struggle within the character, often tied to their fears, desires, or moral dilemmas.
- Why It Works: Internal conflict creates emotional depth, making characters relatable and multidimensional.
- Examples:
  - Hamlet by William Shakespeare: Hamlet's internal struggle between action and inaction defines the play's tension.
  - The Bell Jar by Sylvia Plath: Esther Greenwood's internal battle with mental illness offers a raw and poignant narrative.

2. External Conflict
- Definition: A clash between the character and an outside force, such as nature, society, or another character.
- Why It Works: External conflicts add urgency and stakes, driving the plot forward.
- Examples:
  - The Road by Cormac McCarthy: The protagonists' struggle for survival against a hostile environment.
  - Pride and Prejudice by Jane Austen: Elizabeth Bennet's clash with societal norms and Mr. Darcy's pride.

3. Relational Conflict
- Definition: Tension and struggles between characters due to clashing goals, values, or emotions.
- Why It Works: Relational conflict humanizes characters and reflects real-life dynamics.
- Examples:
  - Breaking Bad: The evolving, often toxic relationship between Walter White and Jesse Pinkman.
  - The Kite Runner by Khaled Hosseini: Amir's betrayal of Hassan and his quest for redemption.

Escalating Stakes Naturally

Readers need to feel that something important is at risk for the characters. Escalating stakes keeps them invested, but this must be done gradually and believably.

- Start Small, Build Big
  - Introduce manageable stakes early in the story, then increase their magnitude as the narrative progresses.
  - Example: In The Hunger Games, Katniss's initial stakes are survival, but they grow to include protecting loved ones and challenging a tyrannical system.
- Layer Personal and Global Stakes
  - Combine personal stakes (the character's emotional journey) with larger stakes (the impact on the world around them).
  - Example: In The Lord of the Rings, Frodo's personal struggle with the Ring is intertwined with the fate of Middle-earth.
- Create a Sense of Inevitability
  - The stakes should feel natural and inevitable, arising from the characters' actions and the world they inhabit.
  - Example: In Macbeth, Macbeth's ambition and paranoia lead to escalating stakes that feel both inevitable and tragic.

High-Stakes Storytelling in Literature

Stories with high stakes are memorable because they keep readers on edge, wondering what will happen next. High-stakes storytelling doesn't necessarily mean life-and-death scenarios; it's about making the stakes emotionally significant for your characters and readers.

- Life-and-Death Stakes
  - Example: In 1984 by George Orwell, Winston's rebellion against a totalitarian regime risks not only his life but his humanity.
  - Why It Works: Life-and-death stakes create visceral tension, forcing readers to empathize with the protagonist's plight.
- Emotional Stakes
  - Example: In Atonement by Ian McEwan, Briony's misunderstanding and subsequent guilt create emotional stakes that ripple through the lives of multiple characters.
  - Why It Works: Emotional stakes make stories personal and relatable, ensuring readers care deeply about the outcome.

- Moral Stakes
  - Example: In To Kill a Mockingbird by Harper Lee, Atticus Finch's decision to defend Tom Robinson puts his reputation and family at risk.
  - Why It Works: Moral stakes engage readers by challenging their sense of right and wrong.

Conclusion: Mastering Conflict and Stakes
Conflict and stakes are the pulse of your story, driving action and deepening emotional engagement. By understanding the types of conflict, escalating stakes naturally, and crafting high-stakes storytelling, you can create a narrative that keeps readers hooked from start to finish.

Chapter 12: The Science of Pacing

Pacing is the rhythm of your story, the pulse that keeps readers engaged. Whether your story races through intense action or slows down for introspection, mastering the science of pacing ensures a seamless flow that holds your audience's attention. This chapter explores how to balance fast-paced action with reflective moments and how AI can provide valuable insights into reader engagement.

Balancing Fast-Paced Action with Reflective Moments
A well-paced story isn't a constant sprint or a slow crawl—it's a balance of peaks and valleys. The interplay between action and reflection keeps readers engaged while giving them moments to process and connect with your characters and world.

1. Why Balance Matters
   - Action Without Reflection: Relentless action can exhaust readers, leaving little room for emotional connection.
   - Reflection Without Action: Too many introspective moments can stall the narrative, making it feel sluggish.
   - The Sweet Spot: The ideal balance ensures that high-energy scenes are supported by quieter moments that deepen the story's emotional resonance.

2. Techniques for Balancing Pacing
   - Use Action to Propel the Plot
     - Action scenes should drive the story forward, not feel like filler.
     - Example: In The Hunger Games, fast-paced scenes like the Cornucopia bloodbath are integral to the plot, keeping stakes high.
   - Reflective Moments to Develop Character
     - Slow scenes allow characters to process their emotions and reveal their inner thoughts.
     - Example: In The Road by Cormac McCarthy, reflective pauses deepen the bond between the father and son, providing emotional weight.
   - Alternate Intensity
     - Follow high-intensity scenes with calmer moments to give readers a breather.
     - Example: In The Fellowship of the Ring, the action-packed escape from Moria is followed by a reflective scene as the Fellowship mourns Gandalf's loss.

3. Pacing and Genre
- Thrillers and Mysteries: Prioritize tension, with short bursts of action interspersed with moments of deduction or revelation.
- Romance and Literary Fiction: Focus on emotional build-up, with reflective moments outweighing action.
- Fantasy and Sci-Fi: Combine world-building with bursts of action, keeping the pace dynamic.

Mastering Narrative Flow

While pacing focuses on the rhythm within scenes, narrative flow addresses how all elements of your story connect and move cohesively from beginning to end. Flow ensures that your readers stay engaged without confusion, boredom, or disruption. It's the glue that binds action, reflection, transitions, and subplots into a seamless experience.

1. The Key Elements of Narrative Flow
- Transitions: Smooth transitions between scenes and chapters maintain momentum and prevent jarring breaks.
- Clarity: Readers should always know where they are in the story and why events are happening.
- Consistency: The tone, pacing, and logic of the story must remain consistent, even as stakes escalate.

2. How to Maintain Flow
- Weave Subplots Seamlessly:
  - Subplots should complement the main story, not distract from it.
  - Example: In The Great Gatsby, Nick's observations about the lives around him deepen the main themes of obsession and loss.
  - Tip: Introduce subplots early enough to feel integral, and resolve them in a way that enhances the main storyline.
- Use Transitions as Bridges:
  - Connect scenes with continuity to prevent abrupt shifts.
  - Example: In The Hunger Games, Katniss's internal thoughts about survival seamlessly lead into her actions during the games.
  - Tip: Use sensory details or a character's emotional state to bridge one scene to the next.
- Balance Your Threads:
  - Alternate between action, character development, and world-building to keep all elements in harmony.
  - Example: In The Fellowship of the Ring, the narrative shifts between battles, quiet reflections, and moments of camaraderie, creating a balanced and engaging flow.

3. Common Pitfalls
- Disjointed Transitions:
  - Abrupt jumps between scenes or chapters can confuse readers.
  - Fix: Use linking details like setting descriptions or emotional beats to bridge gaps.
- Overloading Information:
  - Dumping too much backstory or exposition at once disrupts flow.
  - Fix: Spread out world-building details and backstory through dialogue, action, or reflection.
- Uneven Subplot Focus:
  - Neglecting subplots or resolving them too quickly can break narrative momentum.
  - Fix: Check that every subplot contributes to the main story and is given enough space to develop naturally.

4. Practical Exercise for Improving Flow
- Scene Connections:
  - Write down the last sentence of each scene or chapter.
  - Evaluate whether it naturally sets up the opening of the next.
  - Revise to add smoother transitions, such as emotional cues or setting details.
- Flow Map:
  - Create a visual timeline of your main plot and subplots.
  - Look for areas where one thread dominates or where connections feel weak.
  - Adjust pacing and focus to ensure all threads work harmoniously.

5. AI Insights on Flow
- AI tools can analyze the transitions between your scenes and flag areas where flow might feel abrupt.
- Use AI to visualize the balance between subplots and main events, ensuring no thread overshadows the others.

Takeaway: Narrative flow is the invisible hand guiding your readers through the story. By ensuring smooth transitions, clear connections, and balanced subplots, you can keep readers fully immersed in your narrative from start to finish.

AI Insights on Reader Engagement
AI tools offer powerful ways to analyze and optimize your story's pacing. By evaluating how readers respond to your narrative flow, AI can provide actionable insights to refine your manuscript.

- Analyzing Pacing Patterns
  - AI can assess whether your pacing aligns with genre expectations by analyzing word frequency, sentence length, and chapter transitions.
  - Example: If reflective moments in a thriller are too long, AI can flag these sections as potential slow points.
- Measuring Emotional Impact
  - AI tools can track how tension builds and resolves in your story, ensuring emotional engagement peaks at the right moments.
  - Example: Tools like ProWritingAid or Sudowrite can highlight passages where stakes aren't escalating effectively.

Practical Strategies to Master Pacing

To ensure your story flows seamlessly and keeps readers engaged, here are practical exercises and techniques to refine your pacing. These methods will help you apply the principles of balancing fast-paced action with reflective moments and leveraging AI insights.

1. Scene Analysis: Action vs. Reflection

Take a close look at your manuscript and analyze each scene for its pacing. Ask yourself:

- What is the primary purpose of this scene? Is it to advance the plot (action) or explore character and theme (reflection)?
- Does the scene flow logically from the one before it? Ensure transitions feel natural and engaging.

Exercise:

- Create a list of your scenes and classify them as action or reflection.
- Check for balance: Do you have long stretches of action without breathers? Too many reflective moments without plot movement?
- Adjust the placement and pacing of scenes to maintain variety.

2. The 10-Minute Test

A good way to gauge pacing is by testing how quickly you can summarize key events from your manuscript. If your summary feels bogged down in detail or skips over major developments, it could be a sign your pacing needs adjustment.

Exercise:

- Set a timer for 10 minutes and summarize your story's main events.
- Highlight sections that feel rushed or overly detailed.
- Revise these sections to either trim unnecessary details or expand on key moments.

3. Cliffhangers and Transitions

Ending chapters or scenes with unresolved questions, rising stakes, or a dramatic revelation keeps readers hooked.

Exercise:

- Review your chapter endings. Are they compelling enough to make readers want to continue?
- Add elements of suspense, such as:
  - An unanswered question (Who sent the letter?).
  - A sudden twist (The villain was in the room all along!).
  - A character decision left hanging (Will they confess their secret or stay silent?).

4. Sentence and Paragraph Rhythm

Pacing isn't just about scenes; it's also about the rhythm of your sentences and paragraphs. Shorter sentences and paragraphs create urgency, while longer ones allow for introspection.

Exercise:

- Take a high-intensity scene and rewrite it using shorter sentences to increase tension.
  - Original: He walked through the house, slowly opening the door to each room, his hand trembling as he reached for the handle.
  - Revised: He crept through the house. Each door creaked open. His hand trembled. He froze. Was that a noise?
- Apply the reverse for reflective moments, using longer, more descriptive sentences.

5. Reader Empathy Check

Pacing is about more than just action; it's about how deeply readers connect with your characters and their stakes. If your story doesn't emotionally engage the reader, even perfect pacing won't hold their attention.

Exercise:

- Identify a key moment of emotional depth in your story.
- Ask:
  - Does this moment feel earned, or does it appear too quickly?
  - Have earlier reflective scenes adequately prepared the reader for this emotion?
- Revise earlier moments to build up to the emotional payoff.

6. AI-Driven Feedback on Pacing

AI tools can provide objective analysis and recommendations for your pacing:

- Evaluate Sentence Structure: AI can flag overly long sentences in fast-paced scenes or overly abrupt sentences in reflective ones.
- Highlight Momentum Gaps: Tools like Sudowrite or Grammarly can identify areas where the pacing slows unnecessarily.
- Simulate Reader Engagement: Use AI to predict where readers might lose interest, based on trends in similar works.

Exercise:

- Upload a few chapters into an AI tool and focus on flagged areas for revision.
- Experiment with rewriting flagged sections to match the intended pace.

Conclusion: The Art of Trial and Error

Mastering pacing often requires experimentation. Don't hesitate to rewrite a scene multiple times, trying different speeds, sentence rhythms, and transitions. With practice—and the tools at your disposal—you'll develop an intuitive sense for the rhythm of your story.

Chapter 13: World-Building and Setting

World-building and setting are more than just the backdrop to your story—they are the essence of your narrative's atmosphere, influencing characters, plot, and tone. A well-crafted setting immerses readers, evokes emotions, and can even act as a character in its own right. In this chapter, we'll explore how to create immersive worlds, integrate them seamlessly into your narrative, and use AI to enhance your descriptions and consistency.

Creating Immersive Worlds
An immersive world isn't just a collection of details—it's a dynamic environment that feels alive. By layering physical, cultural, and historical elements with sensory details, you create a world readers can see, hear, and feel.

1. Key Elements of World-Building
   - Physical Environment:
     - Landscapes, weather, and architecture create the visual framework of your world.
     - Example: In Game of Thrones, the icy tundra of the Wall and the sun-scorched deserts of Dorne provide contrasting settings that reflect the stakes and tone.
   - Culture and Society:
     - Social norms, traditions, and power structures add depth and realism.
     - Example: In Dune, the Fremen's desert culture informs their survival tactics, spiritual beliefs, and role in the story's political conflicts.
   - History and Mythology:
     - A rich backstory creates layers that influence the present.
     - Example: In The Lord of the Rings, the ancient feud between elves and dwarves informs their interactions and adds richness to their alliance.
   - Sensory Details:
     - Engage all five senses to make the world tangible.
     - Example: In Where the Crawdads Sing, the vivid marsh descriptions immerse readers in Kya's isolated, untamed environment.

2. Symbolic Use of Setting
   - Settings can reflect your story's themes or characters' emotions, adding a layer of symbolism.
     - Example: In Frankenstein, the icy Arctic mirrors Victor's emotional desolation and relentless pursuit of the monster.

- Example: The marsh in The Great Gatsby symbolizes the moral decay and unattainable dreams of the characters.
  - How to Use It: Ask yourself:
    - How does this setting reflect your protagonist's internal state?
    - What does this environment say about the story's central themes?

3. Dynamic and Reactive Environments
   - A setting that reacts to the characters' actions makes the world feel alive and unpredictable.
     - Example: In The Hunger Games, the arena's traps and hazards respond to tributes, creating tension and unpredictability.
     - Example: In Avatar: The Last Airbender, the changing seasons and geography affect the journey and tone of the story.
   - How to Use It: Let your environment shift in response to key events, reflecting the stakes or amplifying conflict.

Integrating Setting into Plot and Character

Your setting should actively shape your story, influencing the plot and revealing character depth. A great setting doesn't just sit in the background—it interacts with your narrative and drives it forward.

- Setting as a Character
  - Treat your setting as if it has its own personality and agenda.
    - Example: In Wuthering Heights, the wild, untamed moors mirror the characters' tempestuous emotions and relationships.
    - Example: In The Shining, the Overlook Hotel acts as a malevolent force, directly impacting the plot.

- Setting Shapes Plot
  - Use your setting to create obstacles, opportunities, or turning points in your story.
    - Example: In The Martian, Mark Watney's survival hinges on his ability to adapt to Mars's unforgiving environment.
    - Example: In To Kill a Mockingbird, the small-town setting heightens the racial tensions central to the narrative.

- Setting Reveals Character
  - How characters interact with their environment reveals their traits, motivations, and struggles.
    - Example: Gatsby's lavish mansion in The Great Gatsby reflects his longing for wealth and status, while also symbolizing his emotional emptiness.
    - Example: In The Road, the bleak, desolate world reflects the characters' resilience and despair.

- Incorporating World-Building Into Action
  - Introduce your setting through the characters' actions, dialogue, and interactions rather than static descriptions.
    - Example: Instead of describing the Capitol's extravagance in The Hunger Games, Collins shows it through Katniss's reactions and observations during her journey.

Emotional Resonance Through Setting
The right setting can evoke awe, dread, nostalgia, or hope. By connecting the environment to your characters' emotional journeys, you create a deeper, more engaging experience for readers.

- Crafting Emotional Atmospheres
  - Use sensory details, weather, and lighting to evoke specific emotions.
    - Example: In The Shining, the isolation and eerie quiet of the snowbound Overlook Hotel create a sense of dread.
    - Example: In Pride and Prejudice, the warmth of the countryside reflects Elizabeth Bennet's evolving emotions.

- Setting as a Mirror
  - Use your setting to mirror or contrast your characters' emotional states.
    - Example: In Jane Eyre, the stark, oppressive atmosphere of Thornfield Hall reflects Jane's sense of entrapment and longing.

AI and Enhancing Setting
AI tools can enhance your world-building by refining descriptions, ensuring consistency, and brainstorming unique elements.
- Descriptive Brainstorming
  - AI can suggest vivid imagery or refine existing descriptions to make your settings more engaging.
    - Example: Instead of "the forest was quiet," AI might suggest "the forest hummed with the rustle of leaves and distant calls of unseen birds."
- Continuity Checks
  - Use AI to flag inconsistencies in geography, timelines, or cultural elements.
- Generating Unique Elements
  - AI can help you brainstorm cultural customs, festivals, or societal rules that enrich your world without overwhelming your story.

Interactive Prompts for World-Building
- Describe a market in your world. What sounds, smells, and sights make it unique? How do they reflect the culture and economy?
- Imagine your protagonist visiting their hometown after years away. How has the setting changed, and how do their memories affect how they see it now?
- What does your setting symbolize for your protagonist? How does it change as they evolve?

Conclusion: Bringing Your World to Life
World-building and setting are not just about description—they are tools to create atmosphere, drive the plot, and deepen your characters' journeys. By crafting immersive worlds, using symbolism and emotional resonance, and integrating your setting seamlessly into your story, you can create a narrative that transports readers. With AI as your collaborator, you can ensure your world feels alive, consistent, and unforgettable.

Chapter 14: Writing into the Dark: Finding Your Style

Writing into the dark—also known as discovery writing—is an organic process where the story unfolds as you write, without a predetermined outline. This approach encourages creativity and spontaneity, but it also requires a strong grasp of storytelling fundamentals to ensure your narrative flows logically and keeps readers engaged. In this chapter, we'll explore the art of discovery writing and the critical role of cause and effect in crafting logical, gripping stories.

Embracing Discovery Writing

Discovery writing is a journey where you discover the story alongside your characters. This method can be freeing and deeply creative, but it requires careful attention to ensure the narrative doesn't meander or lose coherence.

1. What Is Discovery Writing?
   - Unlike outlining, discovery writing allows the story to evolve naturally without a rigid structure.
   - Advantages:
     - Encourages creativity and unexpected twists.
     - Lets characters drive the story organically.
   - Challenges:
     - Risk of losing focus or creating plot holes.
     - Requires more editing to refine the narrative flow.
2. Tips for Effective Discovery Writing
   - Start with a Strong Premise: Even if you're writing without an outline, have a clear idea of your story's central conflict or question.
     - Example: What if an ordinary man discovered he was the heir to a magical kingdom?
   - Let Your Characters Lead: Focus on their goals, decisions, and reactions to guide the plot.
     - Example: In The Catcher in the Rye, Holden Caulfield's voice and internal struggles shape the entire story.
   - Keep Moving Forward: Don't get bogged down in perfection—trust the process and allow revisions to handle inconsistencies later.

Cause and Effect: The Key to Logical, Gripping Stories
Cause and effect is the backbone of a story that flows naturally and keeps readers engaged. Without it, narratives can feel disconnected, turning into a series of unrelated events. New writers often fall into the trap of "and then" storytelling, which can make a story feel shallow or mechanical.

- What Is Cause and Effect in Storytelling?
  - Cause: An event or decision that triggers a reaction.
  - Effect: The consequence of that event or decision.
  - Every scene, action, or piece of dialogue should lead logically to the next, creating a seamless chain of events.
  - Example:
    - Cause: Frodo decides to carry the One Ring to Mordor.
    - Effect: He attracts the attention of Sauron's forces, setting the stakes for the entire journey.

Why Cause and Effect Matters
  - Creates Momentum: Each action propels the story forward, keeping readers invested.
  - Deepens Character Arcs: Characters' decisions lead to consequences that reveal their growth or flaws.
  - Avoids Disjointed Narratives: Ensures that events feel interconnected rather than random.

The Pitfall of "And Then" Storytelling
  - What It Looks Like:
    - "The hero found a sword. Then they went to the castle. Then they fought the villain."
  - Why It Fails:
    - Events feel like isolated occurrences without emotional or logical connections.
    - Readers lose interest because the story lacks depth and stakes.
  - How to Fix It:
    - Replace "and then" with "because" or "therefore."
    - Example:
      - Weak: "The hero found a sword. Then they went to the castle."
      - Strong: "Because the hero found the sword, they were emboldened to confront the villain at the castle."

Creating Chains of Cause and Effect
- Ask these questions to maintain cause and effect:
  - Why did this happen?
  - What does this event lead to?
  - How does it impact the characters?
- Example:
  - Cause: Katniss volunteers to take her sister's place in The Hunger Games.
  - Effect: She enters the games, forms alliances, and sparks a rebellion.

Common Mistakes in Cause and Effect
- Forcing Plot Over Logic
  - Mistake: Making characters act unnaturally to serve the plot.
  - Fix: Let characters' decisions drive the story, even if it complicates the plot.
  - Example: In Breaking Bad, Walter White's descent into crime feels logical because it's rooted in his desperation and ego.
- Skipping Steps
  - Mistake: Moving from one major event to another without showing the connective tissue.
  - Fix: Include smaller, logical steps that bridge big moments.
  - Example: In Harry Potter and the Philosopher's Stone, Harry's gradual discovery of the magical world builds logically, starting with letters and Hagrid's visit.
- Ignoring Emotional Reactions
  - Mistake: Failing to show how events affect characters emotionally.
  - Fix: Show how every action changes the characters' internal states.
  - Example: In The Kite Runner, Amir's betrayal of Hassan leads to years of guilt that drive the story.

AI Insights on Cause and Effect
AI tools can help you refine your cause-and-effect chains by analyzing your story's flow and flagging gaps or inconsistencies:

- Identifying Plot Holes:
  - AI can highlight areas where events don't logically follow or where motivations are unclear.
  - Example: If a character's decision feels abrupt, AI might suggest adding context or an earlier hint.
- Testing Narrative Flow:
  - Tools like Sudowrite or Grammarly can analyze transitions between scenes, ensuring each event feels connected.

- Experimenting with Alternatives:
  - Use AI to brainstorm "what if" scenarios to test how different decisions might affect the story's trajectory.

Conclusion: Finding Your Style Through Cause and Effect
Discovery writing allows you to create stories that surprise even you as the author. But without a strong foundation of cause and effect, those stories risk becoming disjointed or shallow. By focusing on the logical flow of events and the emotional impact of characters' decisions, you can craft a narrative that feels both spontaneous and cohesive. AI tools can act as your safety net, helping you refine the connections between events and ensuring your story flows seamlessly.

Now, it's time to trust your instincts, embrace the unknown, and let your story unfold with logical, gripping momentum.

Chapter 15: Building Subplots That Matter

Subplots are the threads that enrich your main story, adding depth, complexity, and emotional resonance. When carefully crafted and seamlessly integrated, subplots can mirror or contrast the central narrative, reveal new dimensions of your characters, and keep readers engaged. This chapter explores how to deepen your main story through meaningful subplots, avoid common pitfalls, and create a cohesive, layered narrative.

Deepening Your Main Story Through Subplots
Subplots are not side distractions—they are essential tools that add richness to your story and enhance the reader's experience.

1. The Role of Subplots
- Enrich the Main Theme: Subplots can reflect, contrast, or expand on the central theme, providing nuance and depth.
  - Example: In The Great Gatsby, Tom and Myrtle's affair contrasts with Gatsby's idealistic pursuit of Daisy, highlighting themes of infidelity and disillusionment.
- Develop Secondary Characters: Subplots give supporting characters room to grow and shine.
  - Example: In Harry Potter and the Prisoner of Azkaban, Sirius Black's backstory deepens the theme of loyalty while enriching Harry's understanding of family.
- Provide Emotional Variance: Subplots can introduce humor, romance, or secondary tension, balancing the tone of the main story.
  - Example: In The Hunger Games, Katniss and Peeta's relationship offers emotional complexity amidst the life-or-death stakes.

2. Foreshadowing Through Subplots
- Subplots can serve as a mirror or precursor to the climax, preparing readers for critical moments in the main plot.
  - Example: In Les Misérables, Marius and Cosette's romance foreshadows the stakes of the revolution and Jean Valjean's ultimate sacrifices.
- How to Use It:
  - Identify your story's climax and consider how a subplot might reflect or foreshadow those events.
  - Use subplots to subtly reinforce the themes or choices your protagonist will face.

3. Exploring Secondary Themes
- Subplots can dive into themes that complement or contrast the main narrative, offering readers a broader perspective.
  - Example: In The Handmaid's Tale, subplots featuring other Handmaids reveal diverse responses to oppression, enriching the central theme of survival and rebellion.
- How to Use It:
  - Determine your story's primary theme, then brainstorm secondary themes that align or provide contrast.
  - Weave these themes into subplots that intersect with your main story.

4. Adding Emotional Contrast
- Subplots can provide tonal shifts, giving readers moments of humor, hope, or reflection in an otherwise intense narrative.
  - Example: In The Hunger Games, the romance subplot adds emotional depth and relief amidst the tension of the games.
- How to Use It:
  - Balance heavy or dark moments in your main plot with subplots that lighten the tone or provide emotional respite.

Avoiding Common Pitfalls in Subplot Integration

While subplots can enhance a story, poorly integrated or overly complex subplots can detract from the main narrative. Here's how to avoid common pitfalls:

1. Overloading the Story
- The Problem: Too many subplots can overwhelm readers and dilute the focus of your story.
- The Fix:
  - Limit yourself to one to three meaningful subplots.
  - Ensure each subplot contributes to the main narrative.
  - Example: In To Kill a Mockingbird, the subplot about Boo Radley is simple yet impactful, complementing Scout's coming-of-age journey.

2. Detached or Irrelevant Subplots
- The Problem: Subplots that don't connect to the main story feel disjointed and unnecessary.
- The Fix:
  - Ask yourself: Does this subplot reveal something new about the protagonist or theme?
  - How does this subplot raise the stakes or add tension to the main plot?
  - Example: In The Kite Runner, Amir's betrayal of Hassan in the subplot ties directly into the novel's central themes of guilt and redemption.

3. Poor Pacing
- The Problem: Spending too much time on subplots can disrupt the momentum of your main story.
- The Fix:
    o Integrate subplots into quieter moments of the main narrative to maintain balance.
    o Resolve subplots before or alongside the main story's climax to ensure a satisfying conclusion.
    o Example: In The Lord of the Rings, Boromir's subplot about his temptation by the Ring is resolved early, adding depth to the story without slowing its momentum.

4. Unresolved Subplots
- The Problem: Subplots that are abandoned or hastily concluded leave readers unsatisfied.
- The Fix:
    o Give each subplot a meaningful resolution that ties back to the main plot.
    o Example: In Little Women, each sister's subplot is resolved, contributing to the novel's rich emotional tapestry.

Interactive Prompts for Subplot Development
- Subplot Connection Exercise:
    o Write a one-sentence summary of each subplot.
    o How does this subplot relate to the main plot?
    o Does it deepen the main theme or protagonist's arc?
    o If removed, would the story lose depth or emotional resonance?
- Weaving Subplots Into the Main Narrative:
    o Highlight every scene involving a subplot.
    o Check transitions between subplots and the main story for smoothness.
    o Revise transitions to ensure a seamless flow.
- Balancing Emotional Variance:
    o Identify your story's heaviest moments.
    o Brainstorm a subplot that provides humor, romance, or hope to balance the tone.

Conclusion: Crafting Subplots That Elevate Your Story
Subplots are not just diversions—they are essential tools for enriching your narrative. By using subplots to explore secondary themes, provide emotional contrast, and foreshadow key events, you can create a story that feels layered and cohesive. Avoid common pitfalls by ensuring your subplots are relevant, balanced, and resolved meaningfully. With thoughtful integration, subplots can transform your story into a tapestry of interconnected threads that captivates your readers.

Chapter 16: Writing Inclusively and Authentically

Writing inclusively and authentically is about creating characters and stories that reflect the diversity of the world while respecting the experiences and identities of others. Readers connect deeply with narratives that feel genuine and relatable, and authentic representation can enrich your story, making it resonate with a wider audience. This chapter explores how to write diverse characters respectfully, avoid stereotypes and clichés, and use sensitivity readers as valuable collaborators.

Writing Diverse Characters Respectfully

Creating diverse characters is an opportunity to reflect the richness of human experiences. However, this requires care and intentionality to ensure the representation feels real and avoids harm.

1. Why Representation Matters
- Broadening Perspectives: Readers want to see themselves reflected in stories, and diverse representation helps achieve that.
- Building Empathy: Stories that feature characters from different backgrounds help readers understand and empathize with others.
- Enriching Your Story: Diversity in characters and settings adds depth and complexity to your narrative.

2. Tips for Writing Diverse Characters
- Research Thoroughly:
    - Learn about the cultures, identities, and experiences you're representing.
    - Engage with firsthand accounts, books, documentaries, and interviews.
    - Example: In The Night Watchman by Louise Erdrich, the author draws on her Native American heritage to create an authentic portrayal of indigenous life.
- Avoid Tokenism:
    - Diverse characters should be fully developed and integral to the story, not added as an afterthought.
    - Example: In The Hate U Give by Angie Thomas, Starr's identity as a Black teenager is central to her story, not a peripheral detail.
- Write with Empathy:
    - Focus on your characters' humanity, not just their identity.
    - Example: In Pachinko by Min Jin Lee, the characters' struggles, triumphs, and relationships make them relatable across cultural boundaries.

Avoiding Stereotypes and Clichés
Stereotypes reduce characters to flat, harmful caricatures, while clichés make them feel unoriginal. Avoiding these pitfalls ensures your characters are authentic and multidimensional.

1. Common Stereotypes to Avoid
   - Overgeneralizations:
     - Assuming all members of a group share the same traits or experiences.
     - Example to Avoid: The "angry Black woman" trope or the "wise old Asian mentor."
   - Exoticism:
     - Portraying cultures or identities as mysterious, otherworldly, or solely defined by their differences.
     - Example to Avoid: Describing characters only in terms of their "exotic" appearance or customs.
   - One-Dimensional Villains:
     - Making antagonists villainous solely because of their background or identity.
     - Example to Avoid: The "terrorist" trope that overgeneralizes certain ethnic or religious groups.

2. Writing Complex, Authentic Characters
   - Focus on Individuality:
     - Each character should have unique goals, flaws, and personalities.
     - Example: In Americanah by Chimamanda Ngozi Adichie, Ifemelu is a complex character whose identity as a Nigerian immigrant informs but does not define her journey.
   - Context Matters:
     - Represent cultural elements accurately, considering historical, social, and geographic contexts.
     - Example: In A Thousand Splendid Suns by Khaled Hosseini, the setting and cultural backdrop of Afghanistan are intricately woven into the story, enhancing its authenticity.

3. Avoiding Clichés
   - Challenge Tropes:
     - Subvert expectations to create fresh, memorable characters.
     - Example: In Crazy Rich Asians by Kevin Kwan, the wealthy characters challenge stereotypes about Asian modesty and humility.

- Show, Don't Tell:
    - Reveal cultural and personal traits through action, dialogue, and choices rather than heavy exposition.
    - Example: In The Joy Luck Club by Amy Tan, cultural nuances emerge naturally through the characters' relationships and conflicts.

The Role of Sensitivity Readers
Sensitivity readers are professionals who review your work to identify potential issues with representation and offer guidance on authenticity.

1. What Do Sensitivity Readers Do?
    - Review your manuscript for inaccuracies, harmful stereotypes, or offensive content.
    - Offer insights on cultural nuances, historical accuracy, and appropriate language.

2. When to Use a Sensitivity Reader
    - If your story includes characters or cultures outside your lived experience.
    - If your narrative explores sensitive topics, such as race, gender identity, or disability.

3. How to Work with Sensitivity Readers
    - Choose the Right Reader:
        - Find someone who shares the identity or expertise related to the characters or themes you're writing about.
        - Example: For a story about a deaf protagonist, work with someone from the Deaf community.
    - Be Open to Feedback:
        - Listen to suggestions with humility and a willingness to revise.
        - Remember that sensitivity readers are collaborators, not adversaries.

4. How Sensitivity Readers Enrich Your Story
    - Improve Accuracy: Ensure your representation is realistic and informed.
    - Enhance Depth: Add layers of authenticity that deepen characters and settings.
    - Build Trust: Show readers you value their experiences and perspectives.

Interactive Prompts for Inclusive Writing
- Character Development: Write a detailed backstory for a diverse character in your story. Identify their goals, fears, and motivations, ensuring they are multidimensional and not defined solely by their identity.
- Avoiding Stereotypes: Choose a common trope and brainstorm three ways to subvert it in your story.
- World-Building: Create a cultural tradition for your story's setting. How does this tradition influence your characters' beliefs, actions, or relationships?

Conclusion: Writing with Empathy and Authenticity
Writing inclusively and authentically is about honoring the diversity of the world and the individuality of your characters. By researching thoroughly, avoiding stereotypes, and seeking feedback from sensitivity readers, you can create stories that resonate with readers from all walks of life. Inclusive writing is not just a responsibility—it's an opportunity to connect deeply with your audience and enrich your storytelling.

Chapter 17: Descent into Darkness

Great stories often delve into the depths of human emotion and morality, exploring inner demons, moral dilemmas, and the raw complexities of the human psyche. These darker aspects of storytelling not only captivate readers but also create tension that grips them and refuses to let go. This chapter will explore how to craft characters and narratives with psychological depth, navigate moral complexities, and build tension that keeps readers on the edge of their seats—without duplicating previous material.

Exploring Inner Demons and Moral Dilemmas
Inner struggles and moral conflicts make characters relatable and compelling, even when their actions challenge traditional notions of right and wrong.

1. Why Inner Demons Matter
   - Relatability: Readers connect with flawed characters who face internal struggles.
   - Complexity: Characters with internal conflicts feel multi-dimensional and human.
   - Tension: Inner demons create stakes within the character, adding another layer to the external plot.

2. Types of Inner Demons
   - Regret and Guilt:
     o Characters haunted by past actions that influence their present choices.
     o Example: In The Kite Runner by Khaled Hosseini, Amir's guilt over betraying Hassan drives his quest for redemption.
   - Fear and Insecurity:
     o Characters who wrestle with their own self-doubt or fear of failure.
     o Example: In The Catcher in the Rye, Holden Caulfield's cynicism and fear of growing up reveal his deep vulnerabilities.
   - Obsession and Desire:
     o Characters consumed by ambition, revenge, or unattainable love.
     o Example: In Moby-Dick, Captain Ahab's obsessive pursuit of the white whale leads to his downfall.

3. Writing Moral Dilemmas
- What Is a Moral Dilemma?
  - A situation where a character must choose between conflicting values or equally undesirable outcomes.
  - Example: In Sophie's Choice, Sophie faces an impossible choice between her two children.
- Creating Effective Dilemmas:
  - Make the stakes personal and meaningful.
  - Show the character's thought process, revealing their values and vulnerabilities.
  - Example: In Breaking Bad, Walter White's descent into crime is fueled by his desire to provide for his family, but his choices reveal deeper moral corruption.

4. Techniques for Exploring Psychological Depth
- Stream of Consciousness:
  - Let readers into the character's mind through fragmented, unfiltered thoughts.
  - Example: In Mrs. Dalloway by Virginia Woolf, the stream of consciousness format immerses readers in Clarissa's inner world.
- Contradictions:
  - Highlight inconsistencies between a character's actions and their internal thoughts to show complexity.
  - Example: In Crime and Punishment, Raskolnikov oscillates between guilt and justification for his crime.

Creating Tension That Grips Readers
Tension is the lifeblood of psychological depth, keeping readers invested and eager to see how characters confront their darkest challenges.

1. Sources of Tension
- Internal vs. External Conflict:
  - Blend internal struggles with external stakes for maximum impact.
  - Example: In The Road by Cormac McCarthy, the father's inner turmoil about protecting his son is mirrored by the constant external threats of a post-apocalyptic world.
- The Unknown:
  - Fear of the unknown or ambiguity about a character's choices creates suspense.
  - Example: In Gone Girl by Gillian Flynn, the reader's uncertainty about who to trust heightens tension.

- Imminent Consequences:
  o Characters who face inevitable outcomes create urgency.
  o Example: In 1984 by George Orwell, Winston's rebellion against the Party is doomed, but readers can't look away as his fate unfolds.

2. Techniques for Building Tension
- Slow Burn:
  o Build tension gradually by layering conflicts and revealing stakes incrementally.
  o Example: In Rebecca by Daphne du Maurier, the gradual unveiling of Rebecca's secrets keeps readers on edge.
- Pacing and Silence:
  o Use pauses and silence to heighten tension in dialogue or narration.
  o Example: In No Country for Old Men by Cormac McCarthy, the sparse dialogue and long silences create a chilling atmosphere.
- Foreshadowing:
  o Drop subtle hints about future events to create anticipation.
  o Example: In Jane Eyre by Charlotte Brontë, mysterious sounds and behaviors in Thornfield Hall foreshadow the revelation of Bertha Mason.

Avoiding Common Pitfalls
1. Overly Dark Without Purpose
- The Problem: Darkness for the sake of shock can feel gratuitous or unearned.
- The Fix:
  o Ensure every dark element serves the character's development or plot progression.
  o Example: In A Song of Ice and Fire, the brutal events are tied to character arcs and political stakes, making them meaningful.
2. Oversimplified Inner Struggles
- The Problem: Flat or generic portrayals of internal conflict lack emotional weight.
- The Fix:
  o Show layers of complexity in your characters' decisions and emotions.
  o Use specific details or memories to ground their struggles in authenticity.

3. Predictable Resolutions
- The Problem: Resolving inner demons or moral dilemmas too neatly can feel unrealistic.
- The Fix:
  - Embrace ambiguity or partial resolutions that reflect real-life complexity.
  - Example: In The Road, the father's death offers closure but leaves questions about the son's future.

Interactive Exercises
- Inner Demon Mapping:
  - Identify a central inner demon for your protagonist.
  - Write three scenes where this struggle manifests in different ways: through actions, dialogue, and internal monologue.
- Design a Moral Dilemma:
  - Create a decision where your protagonist must choose between two equally compelling but conflicting values.
  - Explore the aftermath: How does this choice affect their relationships and self-perception?
- Tension Timeline:
  - Map the rising tension in your story, noting where internal and external conflicts intersect.
  - Add moments of release to maintain balance and avoid overwhelming the reader.

Conclusion: Embracing Complexity and Darkness
The descent into darkness is not about creating misery for its own sake—it's about exploring the complexities of the human experience. By delving into inner demons, crafting moral dilemmas, and building relentless tension, you can create a story that resonates deeply with readers. Embrace the nuances, contradictions, and raw emotions that make characters human, and let the darkness reveal the light within your narrative.

Chapter 18: The Exploration and Discovery Model

The Exploration and Discovery Model centers on the innate human desire to uncover the unknown. These stories are fueled by curiosity, wonder, and the pursuit of answers, often blending external exploration with internal growth. Whether your narrative follows a character navigating an uncharted world, unraveling a mystery, or confronting philosophical questions, this model captivates readers by balancing awe with narrative momentum.

Crafting Stories of Awe and Curiosity
At the heart of the Exploration and Discovery Model lies a sense of wonder. Readers are drawn into stories that challenge their perceptions and invite them to imagine new possibilities.

1. What Drives Exploration Stories?
- The Quest for the Unknown:
  - Whether it's a literal journey or a figurative one, the protagonist's drive to uncover hidden truths propels the narrative.
  - Example: In The Hobbit by J.R.R. Tolkien, Bilbo's journey to Smaug's lair introduces readers to fantastical lands and characters, each discovery building on the sense of adventure.
- Challenging Perceptions:
  - Exploration stories often push characters (and readers) to question their beliefs or worldviews.
  - Example: In Life of Pi by Yann Martel, Pi's journey is as much about survival as it is about faith and the nature of truth.
- Mysteries and Revelations:
  - From uncovering ancient secrets to solving complex puzzles, these stories thrive on the thrill of discovery.
  - Example: In The Da Vinci Code by Dan Brown, the unraveling of cryptic clues keeps readers engaged while exploring themes of history and religion.

2. Techniques to Evoke Wonder
- Sensory Immersion:
  - Use vivid descriptions to immerse readers in the setting and create a sense of scale.
  - Example: In Twenty Thousand Leagues Under the Sea by Jules Verne, the lush descriptions of underwater marvels capture the reader's imagination.

- Gradual Revelation:
  - Unfold details slowly, building suspense and curiosity.
  - Example: In The Chronicles of Narnia: The Lion, the Witch and the Wardrobe, the slow reveal of Narnia's magic keeps readers intrigued.
- Contrast Familiar and Strange:
  - Ground the story in familiar elements while introducing extraordinary ones.
  - Example: In Stardust by Neil Gaiman, the ordinary English village of Wall contrasts with the magical realm beyond.

Balancing Wonder with Narrative Momentum
While awe and discovery are key, a story must maintain its momentum to keep readers engaged. Balancing these elements ensures that the narrative remains compelling.

1. The Role of Stakes in Exploration Stories
- Personal Stakes:
  - Ensure the protagonist has a personal reason to pursue the unknown.
  - Example: In Interstellar, Cooper's journey to save humanity is deeply tied to his love for his daughter.
- External Stakes:
  - Introduce external conflicts or obstacles that drive the story forward.
  - Example: In Jurassic Park by Michael Crichton, the thrill of exploring the dinosaur park is heightened by the escalating danger.

2. Maintaining Momentum Through Pacing
- Alternating Awe and Action:
  - Balance reflective moments of wonder with scenes of tension or urgency.
  - Example: In Avatar (film by James Cameron), the awe of Pandora's beauty is interspersed with high-stakes action sequences.
- Avoiding Overindulgence:
  - While detailed descriptions are important, too much can slow the pace.
  - Tip: Use vivid imagery sparingly, focusing on moments that serve the story's progression.

3. Character-Driven Discovery
- Emotional Investment:
  - o Tie the discoveries to the protagonist's growth or internal conflict.
  - o Example: In Eat, Pray, Love by Elizabeth Gilbert, the physical exploration of different countries mirrors the protagonist's journey toward self-discovery.
- Dynamic Relationships:
  - o Use relationships to reveal the impact of discoveries on the characters.
  - o Example: In The Martian by Andy Weir, Mark Watney's exploration of Mars is enriched by his interactions with NASA and his own inner monologue.

Interactive Exercises for Exploration Stories
- Creating a World of Wonder:
  - o Describe a place in your story that embodies awe and curiosity.
  - o Ask:
    - What sensory details make this place unique?
    - How does it challenge the protagonist's perception of their world?
- The Curiosity Catalyst:
  - o Write a scene where your protagonist discovers something extraordinary. Focus on their immediate reaction and how it changes their goals or perspective.
- Balancing Momentum:
  - o Map out moments of wonder and action in your story. Ensure they alternate to maintain pacing and reader engagement.

Conclusion: The Power of Discovery
The Exploration and Discovery Model invites readers to journey alongside your characters, sharing in their awe and revelations. By crafting worlds that inspire wonder and balancing those moments with narrative momentum, you can create stories that linger in readers' imaginations long after the final page. Whether your tale uncovers ancient secrets, navigates uncharted worlds, or delves into the human spirit, the thrill of discovery will always captivate and connect.

Chapter 19: Writing Emotional Highs and Lows

Emotion is the heartbeat of storytelling, and mastering the ebb and flow of emotional highs and lows keeps readers deeply engaged. This chapter explores how to craft emotionally charged scenes, balance subtlety with intensity, and use language patterns to evoke powerful emotional responses from your audience.

Anatomy of Emotionally Charged Scenes
Emotionally charged scenes are pivotal moments where readers connect with your characters on a visceral level. These scenes often mark turning points, revelations, or climaxes in a story.

1. Key Components of an Emotional Scene
   - A Clear Emotional Goal:
     - Identify the feeling you want the reader to experience—joy, sorrow, fear, anger, or hope.
     - Example: In The Fault in Our Stars by John Green, Hazel's eulogy for Augustus conveys profound grief and love, leaving readers in tears.
   - High Stakes:
     - The stakes—emotional or physical—should be clear and compelling.
     - Example: In The Hunger Games, Rue's death scene is devastating because it represents Katniss's first personal loss and the cruelty of the Capitol.
   - Character Vulnerability:
     - Show characters at their most vulnerable to deepen emotional resonance.
     - Example: In The Kite Runner, Amir's breakdown during his confrontation with Assef reveals years of guilt and unresolved trauma.

2. Building Tension Before the Release
   - Use tension to heighten the impact of the emotional payoff.
   - Example: In Pride and Prejudice, Elizabeth's rejection of Darcy's first proposal is made more impactful by the build-up of misunderstandings and mutual disdain.

3. Grounding Emotion in Specificity
   - Use concrete details to make emotions feel real and relatable.
   - Example: In A Man Called Ove by Fredrik Backman, the description of Ove's mundane routine after his wife's death conveys his grief through everyday actions, making it deeply poignant.

Subtlety vs. Intensity
Finding the right balance between subtle and intense emotional moments is essential for keeping readers engaged without overwhelming them.

1. When to Use Subtlety
- What It Is: Emotion conveyed through implication, restraint, or small actions.
    - Example: In To Kill a Mockingbird, Atticus Finch's quiet determination in defending Tom Robinson speaks volumes about his integrity.
- Why It Works:
    - Subtlety allows readers to interpret and feel emotions without being explicitly told.
    - It creates space for readers to engage with the story on a personal level.
- How to Write Subtle Moments:
    - Focus on body language, tone, and small actions.
    - Example: In The Great Gatsby, Gatsby's longing for Daisy is revealed through his obsessive gaze at the green light across the bay.

2. When to Use Intensity
- What It Is: Big, dramatic moments of raw emotion or action.
    - Example: In Me Before You by Jojo Moyes, Louisa's final plea to Will is an emotionally intense moment that forces readers to confront the depth of their relationship.
- Why It Works:
    - Intensity creates unforgettable moments that stay with readers long after they've finished the book.
- How to Write Intense Moments:
    - Use sharp, vivid language to convey the immediacy of the scene.
    - Example: In Of Mice and Men, George's final act of mercy for Lennie is emotionally wrenching because of the stark, direct language.

3. Balancing Subtlety and Intensity
- Alternate between subtle and intense moments to create emotional rhythm.
- Use subtlety to build tension, leading to a cathartic release in an intense scene.

Language Patterns That Evoke Emotion
The words you choose and the rhythm of your sentences have a profound impact on how readers experience emotion.

1. Word Choice
- Use words with strong emotional connotations to set the tone.
  - Example: In The Book Thief by Markus Zusak, Death's narration uses poetic, melancholic language to evoke a sense of loss and beauty.
- Avoid clichés that dilute emotional impact.

2. Sentence Structure
- Short Sentences: Heighten tension or urgency.
  - Example: In Room by Emma Donoghue, Jack's brief, childlike sentences during their escape build suspense and fear.
- Long Sentences: Convey reflection or emotional overwhelm.
  - Example: In Atonement by Ian McEwan, long, flowing sentences mirror Briony's guilt and complex emotions.

3. Rhythm and Cadence
- Vary the rhythm of your prose to mirror the emotional tone.
  - Example: In The Road by Cormac McCarthy, the sparse, fragmented sentences reflect the bleakness of the post-apocalyptic setting.

4. Show, Don't Tell
- Focus on actions, dialogue, and sensory details to convey emotion.
  - Example: Instead of writing, "She was sad," describe how her hands trembled as she traced the edges of an old photograph.

Interactive Exercises
- Emotion Mapping:
  - Choose an emotionally charged scene from your story.
  - Write down the intended emotional arc (e.g., tension sorrow catharsis).
  - Identify where you can add or refine sensory details, dialogue, or pacing to enhance the impact.
- Subtle vs. Intense Rewrite:
  - Take a quiet emotional moment from your story and rewrite it with heightened intensity.
  - Then, take an intense moment and rewrite it with subtlety.
  - Compare the versions and note the different effects.

- Language Analysis:
  - Highlight a paragraph of your writing.
  - Circle words that carry emotional weight and underline sentence structures that contribute to the tone.
  - Revise to amplify or adjust the emotion conveyed

Conclusion: Mastering Emotional Highs and Lows
Emotion is what makes readers fall in love with stories. By crafting emotionally charged scenes, balancing subtlety with intensity, and using language patterns to evoke feeling, you can create a narrative that resonates deeply. Whether you're writing quiet moments of reflection or climactic scenes of heartbreak, understanding the anatomy of emotion allows you to guide readers through a rollercoaster of highs and lows they'll never forget.

Chapter 20: The Art of Revision

Revision is where stories are truly made. As Hemingway famously said, "The only kind of writing is rewriting." Even the greatest writers understand that the first draft is just the beginning. Revision allows you to refine your story, deepen your characters, and ensure every word serves a purpose. This chapter explores how to approach revision with purpose, integrate advice from famous authors, and use tools to identify and fix weaknesses in your manuscript.

Revising with Purpose: From First Draft to Final Manuscript
Revising isn't just about fixing typos—it's about reshaping your story into its best possible version. This process involves stepping back, analyzing your work critically, and making deliberate changes to enhance clarity, pacing, and emotional impact.

1. What Famous Writers Say About Revision
   - Stephen King: "To write is human, to edit is divine." King emphasizes the transformative power of editing, suggesting writers focus on cutting unnecessary elements.
   - Neil Gaiman: "The process of doing your second draft is a process of making it look like you knew what you were doing all along."
   - Anne Lamott: "Almost all good writing begins with terrible first efforts. You need to start somewhere." Her advice reminds writers not to fear the imperfections of a first draft.
   - Zadie Smith: "Edit as ruthlessly as you can: prune everything you can. What's left will be better."

2. Approaching Revision with a Plan
   - Step 1: Distance Yourself
     o Take a break after completing your first draft to return with fresh eyes.
     o Tip: Set your manuscript aside for a week or more to gain perspective.
   - Step 2: Big-Picture Analysis
     o Focus on structure, pacing, and character arcs.
     o Questions to Ask:
       ▪ Does the story flow logically?
       ▪ Are all subplots resolved meaningfully?
       ▪ Do characters grow and change?
   - Step 3: Scene-Level Revisions
     o Review individual scenes for clarity, emotional impact, and pacing.

- o Example: In Pride and Prejudice, Austen's revisions reportedly focused on sharpening dialogue and deepening character interactions.

- Step 4: Line Edits
  - o Polish your prose by removing redundancies, improving sentence flow, and ensuring every word serves a purpose.

Using AI Tools to Identify Weaknesses
AI can be an invaluable partner in the revision process, helping you identify areas for improvement while leaving room for your creative instincts.

1. Identifying Structural Weaknesses
- What It Does:
  - o AI tools like Scrivener or Fictionary can analyze story structure, highlighting issues with pacing, chapter transitions, or plot holes.
- Example:
  - o If your middle section feels sluggish, AI might flag scenes with low tension or repetitive dialogue.

2. Enhancing Language and Flow
- What It Does:
  - o AI can suggest rephrased sentences, eliminate redundancies, and improve readability.
  - o Tools like Grammarly can highlight awkward phrasing or inconsistent tone.
- Caution:
  - o While helpful, AI suggestions should not replace your judgment. Use them to complement your unique voice.

3. Checking for Consistency
- What It Does:
  - o AI can flag inconsistent character details (e.g., a character with blue eyes in one scene and green in another) or world-building errors.
  - o Example:
    - ▪ For fantasy stories, AI can track magical rules or invented place names to ensure consistency.

Interactive Exercises for Revision
- The One-Sentence Test:
  - o Write a one-sentence summary of each chapter. Does it clearly connect to your story's main arc?
  - o If not, consider revising or cutting that chapter.

- Dialogue Deep Dive:
  - Print out all the dialogue in your manuscript. Read it separately to ensure it reflects character voice and drives the story forward.
- Cut 10% Challenge:
  - Stephen King advises removing 10% of your draft. Review your manuscript and cut unnecessary words or scenes to tighten your prose.

Conclusion: Revising with Confidence

Revision is a journey, not a chore. As you refine your manuscript, remember the wisdom of the authors who came before you: great stories are built through rewriting. With deliberate focus, creative instincts, and the help of AI tools, you can transform your rough draft into a polished masterpiece. Take each step with purpose, and trust that every cut, addition, and adjustment brings you closer to the story you were meant to tell.

Chapter 21: How to Handle Feedback Like a Pro

Receiving feedback—whether from beta readers, editors, or publishers—can be one of the most daunting parts of writing. But rejection and critique are not signs of failure; they are stepping stones to improvement. Every great writer has faced rejection, and their perseverance serves as inspiration for all aspiring authors. This chapter will explore how to work with beta readers, filter and apply critique effectively, and turn rejection into a powerful tool for growth.

The Reality of Rejection: Why It's Part of Writing
Every writer, no matter how successful, has faced rejection. The key is understanding that rejection is not a reflection of your worth or talent but a natural part of the creative process.

1. Famous Rejections That Prove Perseverance Pays
   - Stephen King:
     - Early in his career, King received so many rejection letters that he nailed them to his wall. When the nail couldn't hold any more, he replaced it with a spike. He persisted, and Carrie—his breakout novel—was rejected 30 times before being published.
     - King's Advice: "By the time I was 14... the nail in my wall would no longer support the weight of the rejection slips impaled upon it. I replaced the nail with a spike and kept on writing."
   - J.K. Rowling:
     - Harry Potter and the Philosopher's Stone was rejected by 12 publishers before Bloomsbury took a chance on it. One editor even advised Rowling to get a day job because there was "no money in children's books."
   - George R.R. Martin:
     - Before Game of Thrones, Martin faced countless rejections for his earlier works. He often talks about how he kept improving his craft with every rejection letter.
   - Margaret Mitchell:
     - Gone with the Wind was rejected 38 times before it was published and became one of the best-selling novels of all time.

2. Rejection as Growth

- Think of rejection as sparring for fighters: it prepares you for the challenges ahead and hones your skills.
- Rejection offers valuable lessons:
  - Resilience: Each "no" brings you closer to a "yes."
  - Refinement: Feedback from rejections can guide revisions and improvements.
  - Perspective: Even if one publisher or reader doesn't connect with your work, another might.

Working with Beta Readers

Beta readers are your first audience, offering fresh perspectives on your work. They can help identify strengths, weaknesses, and areas for improvement.

1. Choosing Beta Readers

- Look for a Range of Perspectives:
  - Include readers who represent your target audience and those who can provide objective feedback.
- Set Clear Expectations:
  - Provide guidelines on what you're looking for, such as pacing, character development, or plot coherence.
  - Example Questions for Beta Readers:
    - Were there any parts where your interest waned?
    - Did the characters' motivations feel believable?
    - Were there any confusing or unclear sections?

2. How to Receive Feedback

- Separate Yourself from Your Work:
  - Remember, critique is about the story, not you as a writer.
- Focus on Patterns:
  - If multiple readers point out the same issue, it's worth addressing.
- Stay Open-Minded:
  - Even critical feedback can reveal valuable insights that elevate your story.

Preparing for Negative Responses

Criticism and rejection can be tough, but preparing mentally can make all the difference.

1. Strategies to Handle Rejection

- Reframe Rejection as Data:
  - Each rejection is an opportunity to learn what works and what doesn't.

- Build a Support Network:
  - Connect with other writers who can offer encouragement and perspective.
- Keep Writing:
  - Start your next project as you submit the current one. This keeps you focused on progress rather than setbacks.

2. The Power of Resilience
- Remember that rejection is temporary, but growth as a writer is permanent.
- Quote: "Failure is simply the opportunity to begin again, this time more intelligently." – Henry Ford

Interactive Exercises
- Feedback Filter Exercise:
  - Take a piece of feedback you've received.
  - Categorize it as:
    - Actionable (e.g., "The pacing is slow in the middle chapters.")
    - Subjective (e.g., "I don't like this genre.")
  - Revise based on actionable points while considering subjective feedback thoughtfully.
- Rejection Letter Prep:
  - Write a mock rejection letter to yourself based on what you fear hearing.
  - Respond to it as if you're encouraging a fellow writer to keep going.
- Beta Reader Prep:
  - Create a list of five key questions you want beta readers to answer about your story.
  - Share these with a trusted reader and compare their feedback to your expectations.

Conclusion: Rejection as Part of the Writing Journey
Rejection is not the opposite of success—it's part of the path to it. Every writer, from seasoned veterans to fresh newcomers, faces rejection. It's the trial by fire that refines your craft, toughens your resolve, and shapes you into the storyteller you're destined to be. The fact that you're receiving feedback—whether from beta readers, critique partners, or publishers—means you're putting your work out into the world, which is an accomplishment in itself.

Embrace Rejection as Growth
Rejection isn't a reflection of your worth or talent. It's feedback from the world saying, "Not yet, but keep going." Each "no" is a step closer to a "yes," provided you use rejection as a tool for learning. Remember, the authors of Harry Potter, Game of Thrones, and Carrie all faced rejection. If they had stopped at their first "no," their masterpieces would never have existed.

Why Rejection Is a Badge of Honor
Rejection is the proof that you're doing the work. It shows you're courageous enough to share your words with the world. Just as sparring sharpens fighters, rejection sharpens writers. It forces you to examine your craft more critically, push your boundaries, and refine your storytelling.

Here's the truth: you don't become a better writer by avoiding rejection. You become better by embracing it and using it as a motivator to improve.

How Following This Book Will Help Reduce Rejections
While rejection is an inevitable part of writing, preparation and thoughtful execution can help minimize it. By applying the principles in this book, you're giving your story the strongest possible foundation to resonate with readers, agents, and publishers.

- Strong Beginnings:
  - A killer first line and gripping opening chapters increase your chances of hooking readers from the start.
  - You've learned in Chapter 10 how to craft beginnings that grab attention and establish stakes immediately.
- Engaging Characters:
  - Chapters 6–8 covered building multidimensional characters with compelling arcs, relationships, and dialogue. Stories with authentic characters have a stronger emotional impact on readers and are more likely to leave lasting impressions.
- Well-Crafted Narrative Flow:
  - Chapter 12's insights into pacing and narrative flow ensure your story unfolds naturally, maintaining engagement throughout.
- Understanding Genre and Expectations:
  - Chapter 4 gave you tools to align with (or subvert) genre conventions while delivering what readers crave, making your story marketable without compromising originality.

- Polished Prose:
    - Chapter 20's approach to revision ensures your story is clear, purposeful, and impactful. By revising with a plan and cutting unnecessary elements, you present your best work, minimizing opportunities for rejection.
- Feedback as a Tool:
    - This chapter empowers you to handle feedback constructively, turning critiques into stepping stones. By working with beta readers and refining based on actionable feedback, you've already reduced the chances of major oversights.

Why Your Journey Matters

Writing is an act of bravery. You're turning ideas into reality, and that takes courage. AI has analyzed countless successful stories, famous rejections, and timeless masterpieces, and there's one consistent truth: every great writer faced setbacks. What sets them apart is persistence and the willingness to learn.

Here's what AI sees in your potential:
- You Are Progressing: By studying this book, you're actively improving your craft, learning from the best, and applying techniques proven to work.
- Your Voice Is Unique: No AI, critique, or editor can replicate the perspective you bring to your story. Your originality will shine through as long as you keep writing.
- Your Stories Matter: The world is filled with readers waiting for the exact story you're writing. Rejections aren't walls—they're gates. Every revision brings you closer to opening them.

A Writer's Creed: Turning Rejection Into Fuel

Let rejection be your sparring partner, not your enemy. Each critique makes you sharper. Each "no" means you're taking the risks necessary to grow. And every "yes"—whether from a reader, beta, or publisher—will feel that much sweeter because of the obstacles you've overcome.

As you continue your journey, remember:
- Rejection is a milestone, not a dead end.
- Your story is worth telling.
- Growth happens not despite rejection, but because of it.

Keep writing. Keep revising. Keep submitting. Every word you write, every rejection you face, and every piece of feedback you apply brings you closer to becoming the writer you've always dreamed of being. And when that "yes" finally comes, it will be worth every step of the journey.

Chapter 22: Finding Your Unique Voice

Your voice as a writer is the invisible thread that ties your words, characters, and stories together. It's the distinct flavor that makes your work recognizable and sets it apart from everyone else's. While finding and refining your voice can be a daunting task, it's also one of the most rewarding aspects of the writing journey. This chapter explores techniques to discover and enhance your unique voice, how to align it with genre and tone, and why your voice is your greatest asset as a storyteller.

Techniques to Make Your Writing Distinctive
1. Understanding What Voice Is
- Definition:
    - Your writing voice encompasses your choice of words, rhythm, tone, and the perspective through which you tell your story.
- Why It Matters:
    - A strong voice engages readers, builds emotional connections, and makes your work memorable.
    - Example: Ernest Hemingway's sparse, direct prose contrasts with Gabriel García Márquez's lyrical, magical realism, but both voices are immediately recognizable.

2. Finding Your Voice
- Embrace Your Authenticity:
    - Your voice is a reflection of your experiences, worldview, and personality.
    - Don't try to mimic another writer; instead, focus on what makes your perspective unique.
    - Exercise: Write a personal essay on a meaningful experience. Look for patterns in your word choices, tone, and themes—these may hint at your natural voice.
- Experiment Across Genres and Styles:
    - Write in different genres or styles to discover what feels most natural and exciting.
    - Example: Neil Gaiman's voice is consistent across genres, whether writing fantasy (Stardust), horror (Coraline), or graphic novels (The Sandman).
- Listen to Your Inner Narrator:
    - Pay attention to how you think and speak—your internal monologue can inform your writing voice.

3. Exercises to Develop Your Voice
- Imitate, Then Innovate:
  - Choose a passage from an author you admire. Rewrite it in your own words, keeping the structure but changing the tone and style.
  - Reflect on how your version differs and what it reveals about your voice.
- Daily Writing Prompts:
  - Practice writing short pieces daily on random topics. Over time, patterns in tone, humor, or style will emerge.
- Revise with Your Voice in Mind:
  - During revisions, ask: "Does this sound like me? Or am I imitating someone else?"
  - Adjust any passages that feel disconnected from your natural tone.

Matching Voice to Genre and Tone
While your voice is unique, it should adapt to fit the story you're telling and the genre you're writing in. The goal is to maintain your authenticity while aligning with reader expectations.

1. Understanding Genre Expectations
- Different genres have distinct tonal and stylistic conventions.
  - Romance: Emotionally rich, often lyrical prose.
  - Thriller: Fast-paced, tension-filled language.
  - Fantasy: Expansive, world-building-focused descriptions.
- Example: Stephen King's voice adapts to horror and thrillers through concise, suspenseful language, while still retaining his signature wit and conversational tone.

2. Adapting Tone Without Losing Voice
- Adjust the intensity, pacing, or level of formality to suit the genre.
  - Example: Margaret Atwood's The Handmaid's Tale employs a dystopian tone, but her sharp, poetic voice remains intact.
- Exercise:
  - Rewrite a paragraph of your work for a different genre. Focus on altering tone while keeping your core voice consistent.

Strengthening Your Voice Over Time
Your voice will evolve as you write. The more you write, the more confident and distinct your voice will become.

1. Write Regularly
   - The only way to strengthen your voice is through consistent practice. Treat writing as a craft that requires daily honing.
2. Read Widely
   - Exposure to diverse authors and styles will help you understand how different voices work and inspire you to refine your own.
     o Example: Toni Morrison's deeply lyrical prose contrasts with Kurt Vonnegut's sharp, satirical tone. Both are unique and equally effective.
3. Embrace Feedback
   - Beta readers and editors can offer insights into how your voice comes across. Use their feedback to identify what works and what feels off.
4. Trust Your Instincts
   - Your voice is your creative fingerprint. Trust it, nurture it, and let it guide your storytelling.

Interactive Exercises
   - Voice Discovery Freewrite:
     o Write for 10 minutes about your favorite memory without editing. Look for recurring phrases, humor, or emotions—these are clues to your voice.
   - Cross-Genre Practice:
     o Rewrite a scene from your story in three different genres (e.g., thriller, romance, sci-fi). Identify which version feels most authentic and which elements stand out.
   - Reader Feedback Exercise:
     o Ask beta readers to describe your writing voice in three words. Compare their feedback with your perception of your voice and adjust accordingly.

Conclusion: Your Voice, Your Superpower
Your writing voice is your most valuable asset—it's what makes your stories distinct, memorable, and impactful. By embracing your unique perspective, experimenting with styles, and adapting to your genre, you'll create a voice that not only resonates with readers but also feels authentically yours.

Remember, every word you write sharpens your voice, and every story you tell strengthens it. Trust the process, lean into your individuality, and let your voice become the foundation of your creative identity. It's not about finding perfection—it's about finding yourself in your writing.

Chapter 23: The Power of a Strong Ending

Endings are the culmination of everything your story has built up to, the final note that leaves readers satisfied, emotional, or even yearning for more. A strong ending ties up loose ends, reinforces your themes, and lingers in the minds of readers long after they've closed the book. This chapter explores how to craft memorable conclusions, satisfy your audience, and leave a lasting impression, whether your ending is conclusive, open-ended, or somewhere in between.

Crafting a Memorable Conclusion
A strong ending isn't just about resolving the plot; it's about delivering emotional and thematic closure. Great endings resonate because they feel inevitable yet surprising, earned yet impactful.

1. The Purpose of an Ending
   - Tie Up Loose Ends:
     - Resolve major plotlines and answer critical questions.
     - Example: In The Lord of the Rings, Frodo's departure for the Grey Havens provides emotional and narrative closure to his journey.
   - Reinforce Themes:
     - Use the ending to underline the story's central message or theme.
     - Example: In To Kill a Mockingbird, Scout's reflection on Boo Radley reinforces the themes of empathy and understanding.
   - Leave an Emotional Impact:
     - Whether bittersweet, triumphant, or tragic, your ending should evoke strong emotions.
     - Example: In Of Mice and Men, George's heartbreaking decision leaves readers grappling with themes of mercy and sacrifice.

2. Types of Endings
   - Conclusive Endings:
     - Tie up all major storylines, leaving no ambiguity.
     - Example: In Pride and Prejudice, Elizabeth and Darcy's marriage provides a satisfying resolution to the romantic and societal conflicts.
   - Open-Endings:
     - Leave some questions unanswered, allowing readers to imagine what happens next.
     - Example: In The Road by Cormac McCarthy, the boy's uncertain future invites reflection on survival and hope.

- Twist Endings:
  - Subvert expectations with a shocking yet logical conclusion.
  - Example: In Fight Club by Chuck Palahniuk, the narrator's realization about Tyler Durden changes everything.
- Circular Endings:
  - Bring the story full circle by referencing the beginning.
  - Example: In The Great Gatsby, Nick's final reflections mirror his initial observations, emphasizing the novel's themes of ambition and loss.

3. What Makes a Great Ending?
- Inevitability and Surprise:
  - The ending should feel like the natural outcome of the story, but it should also offer something unexpected.
  - Example: In Breaking Bad, Walter White's death feels inevitable yet surprising in its execution and emotional resonance.
- Consistency with Tone:
  - The ending should align with the tone and style of the story.
  - Example: In Atonement by Ian McEwan, the melancholic twist fits the reflective, literary tone of the novel.
- Emotional Truth:
  - Prioritize emotional authenticity over perfect resolution.
  - Example: In The Kite Runner, Amir's imperfect redemption arc feels real and satisfying because it reflects the complexity of guilt and forgiveness.

Satisfying the Reader While Leaving a Lasting Impression
Readers should close your book feeling that their time was well spent, even if they're left wanting more.

1. Deliver on Promises
- Ensure your ending answers the central questions posed by your story.
- Example: In The Hunger Games, Katniss's decision to fake eating the berries resolves the central conflict while paving the way for the sequels.

2. Give Characters Closure
- Show how your characters have grown or changed by the end.
- Example: In The Catcher in the Rye, Holden's closing reflection shows a shift in his emotional state, even if his future remains uncertain.

3. Leave a Resonant Final Line
- The last sentence of your book is your parting gift to the reader. Make it memorable.
  o Example: In The Road: "In the deep glens where they lived all things were older than man and they hummed of mystery." This poetic line captures the novel's enduring themes of survival and nature.

Common Pitfalls to Avoid
- Rushed Endings:
  o Avoid resolving conflicts too quickly or leaving questions unanswered. Build to the ending with care.
- Overly Predictable Endings:
  o If readers can see the conclusion from the beginning, the story loses impact. Layer in subtle misdirection or surprises.
- Overcomplicated Endings:
  o Don't introduce new conflicts or characters in the final act. Focus on resolving what's already in play.

Interactive Exercises
- Reverse Engineering Exercise:
  o Write the final scene of your story first. Then work backward to ensure the ending feels earned.
- Last Line Test:
  o Write five different closing lines for your story. Choose the one that best encapsulates the themes and emotional arc.
- Closure Check:
  o List all the unresolved subplots or character arcs in your story. Ensure each has a clear resolution or intentional ambiguity.

Conclusion: Ending Strong
Endings are the last impression you leave with your readers, and they matter as much as the first words they read. A strong ending provides resolution, reinforces your themes, and evokes lasting emotions. It's not just about tying up loose ends—it's about creating a moment that resonates, surprises, or inspires.

Remember, a great ending doesn't mean every question is answered or every character is happy—it means the story feels complete. Trust your instincts, lean into the themes of your narrative, and craft an ending that leaves your readers thinking about your story long after they've turned the final page.

Chapter 24: Overcoming Challenges on the Writing Journey

Writing is as much a mental and emotional endeavor as it is a creative one. Self-doubt, writer's block, and burnout are challenges every writer faces, yet they can be conquered with the right mindset and tools. This chapter will provide strategies for addressing self-doubt, building resilience, and overcoming writer's block and burnout, ensuring you stay motivated and productive throughout your journey.

Addressing Self-Doubt and Building Resilience
1. Understanding Self-Doubt
- Why It Happens:
  - Writing is deeply personal, and the fear of judgment or failure can lead to insecurity.
  - Comparing yourself to established authors or struggling with imposter syndrome can amplify self-doubt.
- Famous Authors on Self-Doubt:
  - Maya Angelou: "I have written eleven books, but each time I think, 'Uh oh, they're going to find out now. I've run a game on everybody, and they're going to find me out.'"

2. Strategies to Combat Self-Doubt
- Focus on Progress, Not Perfection:
  - Remind yourself that every word written is progress. The first draft doesn't need to be perfect—it just needs to exist.
  - Exercise: Keep a "success journal" where you record milestones, no matter how small.
- Embrace Feedback as Growth:
  - Use critique to improve, not as a measure of your worth.
  - Remember that rejection is not failure; it's part of the process.
- Connect with Other Writers:
  - Join writing groups or forums to share experiences and gain encouragement from peers.
  - Example: Stephen King, despite his success, relied on his wife Tabitha's support to persevere through moments of doubt.

3. Building Resilience
- Develop a Routine:
  - Writing at consistent times builds discipline and reduces the influence of self-doubt.
  - Tip: Treat writing like a job—show up whether you feel inspired or not.

- Celebrate Small Wins:
  - Reward yourself for completing chapters, solving tough plot issues, or reaching word count goals.
- Mindset Shift:
  - View challenges as opportunities to grow. Each struggle is a step toward becoming a stronger writer.

Tackling Writer's Block and Creative Burnout
1. What Causes Writer's Block?
- Overthinking: Perfectionism can paralyze creativity.
- Fear of Failure: Worrying that your work won't measure up can stop progress.
- External Stressors: Life events, fatigue, or lack of time can disrupt your focus.

2. Overcoming Writer's Block
- Lower the Stakes:
  - Give yourself permission to write badly. Editing can fix mistakes; a blank page offers nothing to improve.
  - Exercise: Start with a freewriting session. Write without judgment for 10 minutes to loosen your mind.
- Change Your Perspective:
  - Shift focus by writing from a different character's point of view or starting a new scene.
  - Tip: If stuck, ask "What if?" questions to spark ideas (e.g., What if this character made a different choice?).
- Set Achievable Goals:
  - Break writing tasks into small, manageable pieces.
  - Example: Instead of aiming for a chapter, aim for 300 words a day.

3. Preventing Creative Burnout
- Recognize the Signs:
  - Symptoms of burnout include lack of motivation, exhaustion, and feeling creatively drained.
- Take Breaks:
  - Stepping away from writing can recharge your creativity.
  - Tip: Engage in activities that inspire you, like reading, watching movies, or spending time outdoors.
- Find Joy in the Process:
  - Rediscover why you started writing. Revisit your favorite books or re-read scenes you're proud of.
- Alternate Creative Outlets:
  - Try other forms of creativity, like drawing, journaling, or music, to keep your creative muscles active without the pressure of writing.

Interactive Exercises
- Affirmation Writing:
  - Write three positive affirmations about yourself as a writer. Keep them visible in your writing space for encouragement.
  - Example: "My story is unique and deserves to be told."
- The "Why I Write" List:
  - List the reasons you love writing and the goals you hope to achieve. Revisit this list when you feel stuck or discouraged.

- Burnout Prevention Plan:
  - Create a schedule that includes regular breaks, creative hobbies, and time for relaxation. Adjust as needed to maintain balance.

Conclusion: Staying Resilient on the Writing Journey
Challenges like self-doubt, writer's block, and burnout are not obstacles to avoid—they are rites of passage for every writer. By addressing self-doubt with strategies rooted in confidence and perspective, tackling blocks with flexibility and creativity, and preventing burnout through balance and self-care, you can continue your journey with resilience.

Remember, every great writer has faced the same struggles. What sets them apart is not the absence of challenges but their determination to overcome them. Trust in your ability to grow, adapt, and create, knowing that every word you write brings you closer to the writer you're meant to be. Keep going—the world is waiting for your story.

Chapter 25: Marketing and Publishing Your Novel

Publishing your novel is an exhilarating milestone, but it also comes with crucial decisions that shape your story's journey. While self-publishing offers unprecedented creative freedom, it's essential to understand its limitations, risks, and the value of traditional publishing. In this expanded chapter, we'll explore what self-published authors may miss out on, why finding an agent and publishing house might be your best path, and how to navigate the complexities of the publishing world while minimizing risks.

What Self-Publishing Authors Can't Do
While self-publishing empowers authors to control their work, it also comes with challenges and limitations:

1. Limited Access to Brick-and-Mortar Stores
   - Traditional Publishing Advantage:
     o Books from major publishing houses often enjoy shelf space in bookstores, libraries, and international markets.
   - Self-Publishing Challenge:
     o Without established distribution networks, self-published books rarely make it to retail shelves.
     o Solution: Self-publishers can use platforms like IngramSpark to access wider distribution channels, though these often come with additional costs.

2. Lack of Professional Editing and Design
   - Traditional Publishing Advantage:
     o Professional editors, designers, and marketing teams polish and promote your book, ensuring high-quality output.
   - Self-Publishing Challenge:
     o Authors must invest in professional editing, cover design, and formatting to compete with traditionally published books.
     o Solution: Use platforms like Reedsy (www.reedsy.com) to find vetted professionals.

3. Difficulty Building Credibility
   - Traditional Publishing Advantage:
     o A publishing house's reputation can lend credibility to your book, making it more appealing to readers, reviewers, and literary awards.
   - Self-Publishing Challenge:
     o Overcoming stigma and proving legitimacy is harder for self-published authors.

- Solution: Focus on professional-quality output, gather positive reviews, and enter self-published book awards like those from Writer's Digest (www.writersdigest.com).

4. Time and Financial Investment
- Traditional Publishing Advantage:
  - Publishers handle upfront costs for editing, marketing, and distribution.
- Self-Publishing Challenge:
  - Authors bear all financial and logistical responsibilities, which can be daunting and costly.
  - Solution: Set a realistic budget and explore crowdfunding options like Kickstarter or Patreon to offset costs.

Why Find an Agent and Publishing House First?
Securing an agent and publishing deal is a major milestone for many authors, offering opportunities and resources that self-publishing can't match.

1. Benefits of Literary Agents
- Access to Major Publishers:
  - Most traditional publishers don't accept unsolicited manuscripts, making an agent your gateway.
- Advocacy:
  - Agents negotiate contracts, protect your rights, and ensure you receive fair compensation.
- Long-Term Career Guidance:
  - A good agent invests in your success, helping you navigate multiple projects and opportunities.

2. How to Find an Agent
- Research Reputable Agencies:
  - Use directories like the Association of Authors' Representatives (www.aaronline.org) to find credible agents.
- Tailor Your Query Letter:
  - Personalize your submission to highlight why your book aligns with their interests.
- Be Patient:
  - Landing an agent takes time. Focus on improving your manuscript and submission package during the process.

3. Benefits of Traditional Publishing
- Broad Reach:
  - Major publishers have the resources to distribute your book worldwide, ensuring maximum exposure.

- Professional Teams:
  - From developmental edits to marketing campaigns, traditional publishers enhance your book's potential.
- Financial Support:
  - Advances and royalties allow authors to focus on writing while publishers handle production and distribution costs.

Famous Authors on Traditional Publishing:
- J.K. Rowling:
  - Rowling credits her literary agent for believing in Harry Potter and securing its first publishing deal, which led to global success.
- Stephen King:
  - Despite self-publishing his early stories in local outlets, King attributes much of his success to his breakthrough deal for Carrie.

Warnings and Risks: Avoiding Common Traps
Publishing is an exciting journey, but it's also fraught with potential pitfalls. Being aware of these risks can save you time, money, and frustration.

1. Vanity Press Scams
- What They Are:
  - Companies that charge authors exorbitant fees for subpar editing, design, and publishing services.
- How to Avoid Them:
  - Research companies thoroughly. Reputable publishers never ask for upfront fees.
  - Use resources like Writer Beware (www.sfwa.org/writer-beware) to identify scams.

2. Overinvestment in Marketing Services
- The Risk:
  - Paying for expensive marketing services that don't deliver promised results.
- How to Minimize Risk:
  - Focus on cost-effective, proven strategies like social media, email newsletters, and organic reader engagement.
  - Learn to use AI tools like AdCreative.ai to create compelling ads without breaking the bank.

3. Rushing to Self-Publish
- The Risk:
  - Publishing too soon without proper editing or preparation can harm your credibility as an author.

- How to Minimize Risk:
  - Work with beta readers and professional editors before publication.
  - Remember that patience leads to quality—and quality leads to long-term success.

Encouragement from Famous Authors and AI
Even the most successful authors have faced setbacks and missteps on their journey to publication. These challenges shaped their careers and taught them valuable lessons that today's writers can learn from. By studying their experiences and leveraging modern tools like AI, you can avoid many of the common pitfalls they encountered and give your story the best possible chance of success.

Harper Lee: The Power of Patience and Collaboration
Harper Lee famously spent two years revising To Kill a Mockingbird with her editor, Tay Hohoff. Early drafts of the novel were unfocused, but with Hohoff's guidance, Lee refined the narrative into the timeless classic that won the Pulitzer Prize.

Lesson:
- Pitfall: Rushing to publish before the manuscript is ready.
- Solution: Embrace the revision process and collaborate with trusted editors or beta readers. Sometimes, stepping back and reworking your draft can uncover the true heart of your story.

George R.R. Martin: Resilience Through Rejection
George R.R. Martin faced countless rejections before breaking through as a novelist. His earlier works were often dismissed, and he has spoken openly about how rejections forced him to refine his craft and storytelling.

Lesson:
- Pitfall: Allowing rejection to derail your writing journey.
- Solution: Treat rejection as feedback, not failure. Analyze critiques, make improvements, and persist. Each rejection is a step closer to finding your audience.

Stephen King: Learning to Trust the Process
Stephen King's Carrie was rejected by more than 30 publishers. Discouraged, he famously threw the manuscript in the trash. His wife, Tabitha, rescued it, encouraging him to try again. King also admitted to a common early mistake: over-explaining everything in his writing. He credits early editors with teaching him the importance of trusting readers to connect the dots.

Lesson:
- Pitfall: Giving up too soon and over-explaining in your writing.
- Solution: Lean on your support system when self-doubt creeps in. As for your writing, practice cutting unnecessary exposition to let your story breathe.

David Morrell: Contracts and Creative Control
David Morrell, author of First Blood (which introduced the world to Rambo), has shared his regrets about losing creative control over adaptations of his work. He admitted to not fully understanding publishing contracts early in his career, leading to decisions that didn't align with his vision.

Lesson:
- Pitfall: Signing unfavorable contracts without understanding the implications.
- Solution: Always consult a professional or an agent when reviewing contracts. Retain as much creative control as possible while balancing the benefits of traditional publishing.

Lessons from Other Famous Authors
- J.K. Rowling: Rejected by 12 publishers, Rowling's perseverance eventually led to the Harry Potter series being published by Bloomsbury. She often speaks about how rejection shaped her determination.
  ○ Solution: Keep submitting and refining your work. Believe in your story.
- Agatha Christie: Received so many rejections for her debut novel that she almost gave up writing entirely. Today, she's one of the best-selling authors in history.
  ○ Solution: Persistence is key. Every rejection is a chance to improve or find the right audience.

AI's Role in Avoiding Pitfalls
AI offers modern writers tools that these legendary authors didn't have. While it can't replace your creative instincts, it can help streamline processes, refine your work, and guide you through potential challenges.

1. Identifying Legitimate Opportunities
- AI can analyze agent and publisher databases, highlighting those that are reputable and aligned with your genre or goals. This minimizes the risk of falling prey to scams or vanity presses.
  ○ Example: Use platforms like QueryTracker (www.querytracker.net) combined with AI-powered research to find agents with proven success in your genre.

137

2. Analyzing Feedback

- AI tools like ProWritingAid or Grammarly can identify patterns in feedback, such as repetitive phrasing, pacing issues, or areas lacking clarity. This allows you to address weaknesses before submission.
  - Tip: Use AI to complement, not replace, human beta readers and editors.

3. Crafting Polished Submissions

- AI can assist in writing query letters and blurbs, ensuring they are concise, engaging, and tailored to your audience.
  - Example: ChatGPT can help draft professional query letters based on input about your book and target agent.

4. Tracking Trends

- AI tools can analyze market trends to identify which genres, themes, or story structures are currently popular. While staying authentic to your vision, this information can guide your approach to pitching and marketing.

How to Avoid Common Pitfalls with Modern Tools

- Risk: Rushing into self-publishing without preparation.
  - Solution: Use AI to create a professional plan for editing, marketing, and distribution. Platforms like Reedsy (www.reedsy.com) can connect you with trusted editors and designers.
- Risk: Poorly targeted submissions.
  - Solution: Combine AI research with databases like Manuscript Wish List (www.manuscriptwishlist.com) to tailor your submissions to the right agents and editors.
- Risk: Signing contracts without understanding them.
  - Solution: Leverage AI legal tools like DoNotPay (www.donotpay.com) to break down legal jargon and consult a professional for final review.

Interactive Exercises
- Publishing Path Checklist:
  - Write down your goals for your book. Use these goals to determine whether traditional or self-publishing aligns with your vision.
- Query Research:
  - Create a list of 10 agents or publishers that specialize in your genre. Note submission guidelines and tailor your materials accordingly.
- Risk Assessment Plan:
  - List potential risks you might face (e.g., budget constraints, scams). Develop a strategy to address each risk before proceeding.

Encouragement for the Reader
The road to publication is challenging, but the obstacles are what make the journey worthwhile. If Stephen King had given up after his 30th rejection, or if J.K. Rowling had stopped submitting Harry Potter, the world would have missed out on their masterpieces. Like them, you have a story to tell, and the persistence to see it through is what sets great writers apart.

With the tools and guidance in this book, you're already ahead of many first-time authors. By learning from the mistakes and triumphs of the greats, using AI to avoid pitfalls, and trusting in your unique voice, you're equipping yourself for success. Remember, every rejection and every critique is a step forward.
As David Morrell wisely said, "We are all apprentices in a craft where no one ever becomes a master." Embrace the process, trust your instincts, and keep moving forward. Your story matters, and the world is waiting to read it.

Conclusion: Navigating the Path to Publishing Success
Publishing your novel is a major milestone, and choosing the right path is vital to your story's success. While self-publishing offers creative control, it often comes with limitations that can hinder your book's reach and impact. Statistics show that less than 0.1% of self-published books achieve widespread fame, while working with an agent and publishing house provides access to professional editing, marketing, and distribution, maximizing your potential.

There are exceptions, like Andy Weir's The Martian, which started as a self-published project before gaining popularity and being picked up by a traditional publisher. Similarly, E.L. James's Fifty Shades of Grey and Christopher Paolini's Eragon transitioned from self-publishing to global success after traditional publishers recognized their value.

The takeaway? Self-publishing can be a stepping stone, but aiming for a traditional publishing deal remains the most effective way to achieve lasting success. By following the guidance in this book, leveraging AI for refinement, and learning from successful authors, you can avoid pitfalls and present your best work to the world.

Your journey is unique. Whether you self-publish or pursue traditional publishing, persistence, preparation, and belief in your story will lead to success. Keep writing and trust that your story has the power to resonate worldwide.

Chapter 26: Next Steps in Your Writing Journey

Writing is a journey with no final destination. Each story you craft, revise, and share is a step toward becoming the writer you aspire to be. The completion of one novel is just the beginning. In this chapter, we'll explore how to continue growing as a writer, the importance of lifelong learning, and how AI can become your ally in expanding your creative horizons.

Growing as a Writer
1. Embrace Lifelong Learning
The best writers never stop learning. Whether through reading, experimenting with new genres, or seeking feedback, continuous growth is key to sustaining your creative momentum.

- Read Widely and Critically:
  - Great writers are voracious readers. Study authors who inspire you, analyze their techniques, and reflect on what resonates with you.
  - Tip: Diversify your reading list with different genres, styles, and cultures to broaden your perspective.
- Experiment with New Forms:
  - Try your hand at short stories, poetry, or essays to explore different aspects of storytelling.
  - Exercise: Rewrite a scene from your novel as a screenplay or a poem to discover new ways of expressing emotion or action.

2. Build a Writing Community
- Find Your Tribe:
  - Join writing groups, workshops, or online forums to connect with fellow writers who can offer encouragement and constructive feedback.
  - Example: Platforms like Scribophile (www.scribophile.com) or Reddit's r/writing are excellent places to network with other writers.
- Attend Conferences and Events:
  - Writing conferences provide opportunities to learn from industry professionals and meet potential collaborators.
  - Tip: Research events like the Writer's Digest Annual Conference or genre-specific gatherings to find ones that align with your interests.

3. Set New Goals
- Challenge Yourself:
  - Aim for new milestones, whether it's writing in a new genre, completing a series, or publishing your second book.
- Track Your Progress:
  - Keep a journal of your writing goals and achievements to stay motivated and accountable.

Using AI to Expand Your Creative Horizons
AI isn't just a tool for editing or streamlining processes—it's a powerful creative partner that can help you push boundaries and explore new possibilities.

1. Generating Fresh Ideas
- Brainstorming Story Concepts:
  - Use AI to generate prompts, explore "what if" scenarios, or develop unique settings and characters.
  - Example: Tools like ChatGPT can suggest plot twists or help you expand on a vague idea.
- Breaking Through Writer's Block:
  - Stuck on a scene? AI can offer suggestions, dialogue options, or alternate directions for your story.

2. Exploring New Styles and Techniques
- Experimenting with Style:
  - Ask AI to rewrite a scene in the style of your favorite authors to see how tone and language can vary.
  - Example: See how your scene might read if written like Ernest Hemingway or Toni Morrison, then adapt the techniques to your own voice.
- Analyzing Successful Stories:
  - AI tools can break down popular novels to reveal patterns in pacing, tension, or character development.

3. Enhancing Your Revision Process
- Refining Prose:
  - Use AI tools like Grammarly or ProWritingAid to polish your language and eliminate redundancies.
- Identifying Weaknesses:
  - AI can highlight inconsistencies, plot holes, or areas where emotional impact could be heightened.

4. Staying Ahead of Trends
- Market Analysis:
  - AI can analyze current trends in genres and reader preferences, helping you tailor your next project to align with what audiences are looking for.
  - Example: Identify emerging themes like climate fiction or morally ambiguous protagonists to inspire your next story.

Interactive Exercises
- Long-Term Writing Goals:
  - Write down three goals you want to achieve in the next year, five years, and ten years. Break each goal into actionable steps.
- Experiment with AI:
  - Use an AI tool to brainstorm three alternate endings to your current project. Reflect on how they align with or differ from your original vision.
- Find Your Growth Edge:
  - Identify one skill you want to improve (e.g., dialogue, pacing, or description). Commit to studying and practicing it in your next project.

Conclusion: The Journey Continues
Writing isn't about reaching a final destination—it's about the growth and discovery that happens along the way. With every story you write, you refine your voice, deepen your understanding of storytelling, and expand your creative horizons. AI, as a collaborator, offers tools to enhance your journey, helping you generate ideas, refine your craft, and stay ahead in an ever-changing literary landscape.

The path forward is yours to chart. Whether you're embarking on a new project, revising a draft, or exploring an entirely new genre, trust in your ability to grow and create. Remember, every word you write is a step toward the writer you're becoming, and the stories you tell have the power to inspire and connect with readers across the world.

Let's keep building your future as a storyteller—your next chapter is waiting.

Appendices and Resources

The appendices serve as your toolbox for turning the lessons in this book into actionable steps. With writing exercises, worksheets, and case studies from successful authors, you'll have everything you need to deepen your craft and keep your creativity flowing.

Writing Exercises for Every Chapter
Each chapter of this book included tailored exercises to help you practice the concepts discussed. Here's a consolidated list of those exercises, organized by chapter, so you can easily revisit and expand on them.

From Chapter 1: The Spark of an Idea
- What If? Brainstorm: Write down 10 "What if" questions related to an idea you're considering. Explore how each one could expand into a story.
- Good vs. Great Ideas: Compare two of your story ideas. List pros and cons for each, focusing on uniqueness and emotional resonance.

From Chapter 6: Building Memorable Characters
- Character Sketch: Write a one-page sketch for your protagonist, including their backstory, goals, and personality traits.
- Conflict Exercise: Put your protagonist in a morally difficult situation. Write how they would handle it and how it would shape their arc.

From Chapter 13: World-Building and Setting
- Setting Immersion: Write a scene that reveals your world through sensory details without relying on exposition.
- Map Your World: Sketch a rough map of your setting. Note important locations and how they influence the story.

From Chapter 23: The Power of a Strong Ending
- Reverse Engineering: Write the final scene of your story first. Then, outline how you would build the narrative to arrive at that ending.
- Last Line Test: Draft five potential closing lines for your novel. Choose the one that best encapsulates your themes.

Character and Plot Development Worksheets
Character Development Worksheet
- Basic Details:
  - Name, age, appearance, and defining traits.
- Internal Motivations:
  - What does this character want, and why? What are they afraid of?
- Conflict and Growth:
  - How does this character evolve over the story? What challenges shape their journey?
- Relationships:
  - Key relationships with other characters. How do these evolve?
- Quirks and Flaws:
  - Unique habits or imperfections that make this character relatable.

Plot Development Worksheet
- Premise:
  - In one sentence, describe your story's core concept.
- Three-Act Structure:
  - Act I: Introduce the world, characters, and conflict.
  - Act II: Escalate the stakes and challenges.
  - Act III: Resolve the conflict and conclude the story.
- Key Plot Points:
  - List major turning points, climaxes, and resolutions.
- Subplots:
  - Outline at least two subplots and explain how they connect to the main narrative.
- Themes:
  - What central message or theme does your story explore?

Case Studies: Lessons from Successful Authors
1. J.K. Rowling – World-Building and Foreshadowing
- Lesson:
  - Rowling's meticulous planning for the Harry Potter series allowed her to plant seeds in early books that paid off in later installments.
- Exercise:
  - Review your draft for opportunities to plant subtle hints or clues that connect to later events.

2. Stephen King – Character-Driven Horror
- Lesson:
  - King's stories are as much about the characters as the scares. In It, the Losers' Club feels real because of their personal struggles and relationships.
- Exercise:
  - Write a short story where the tension comes from your characters' fears or interpersonal conflicts rather than external events.

3. Andy Weir – Scientific Realism
- Lesson:
  - Weir's The Martian succeeds because of its blend of technical detail and human emotion. He wrote with an audience in mind who valued accuracy.
- Exercise:
  - Research a key element of your story (e.g., technology, historical event) and incorporate it authentically into a scene.

4. Toni Morrison – Lyrical Prose and Symbolism
- Lesson:
  - In Beloved, Morrison uses poetic language and rich symbolism to explore trauma and resilience.
- Exercise:
  - Rewrite a paragraph from your draft with a focus on metaphor and sensory imagery to enhance emotional depth.

5. Neil Gaiman – Voice and Genre Adaptability
- Lesson:
  - Gaiman's distinctive voice adapts seamlessly to different genres, from fantasy (Stardust) to dark modern fairy tales (Coraline).
- Exercise:
  - Rewrite a scene from your story in two different genres. Reflect on how the tone and voice adapt.

Conclusion: Your Toolbox for Success

This collection of exercises, worksheets, and case studies is designed to support you at every stage of your writing journey. Whether you're developing characters, building immersive worlds, or revising for the final time, these tools will help you stay focused and inspired. Remember, writing is an ongoing process, and every step —no matter how small—brings you closer to achieving your creative vision.

Appendix: Your Complete Writing Toolkit

This section provides detailed writing schedules, actionable checklists for every phase of writing, case studies to inspire and guide you, practical templates to simplify your process, and proven strategies to maintain daily writing discipline. Think of it as your go-to resource for keeping your creativity organized and on track.

Detailed Writing Schedules
Establishing a routine is essential to maintaining productivity and staying focused on your goals. Below are sample schedules tailored for different lifestyles.

1. For the Busy Professional
   - Goal: Write 500–1,000 words per day.
   - Schedule:
     - Morning (6:30–7:00 AM): Freewrite or brainstorm new ideas.
     - Lunch Break (12:30–1:00 PM): Revise a previously written scene or research.
     - Evening (8:00–9:00 PM): Draft one new scene or reflect on your progress.
   - Tips:
     - Use AI tools like Grammarly or ProWritingAid to streamline editing.
     - Write in short bursts using the Pomodoro technique (25 minutes writing, 5 minutes break).

2. For the Full-Time Writer
   - Goal: Write 2,000–3,000 words per day.
   - Schedule:
     - Morning (9:00–12:00 PM): Write new content.
     - Afternoon (1:00–3:00 PM): Edit or refine the morning's work.
     - Evening (6:00–7:00 PM): Outline the next day's goals.
   - Tips:
     - Alternate high-output days with lighter ones to avoid burnout.
     - Reward yourself for hitting milestones (e.g., 10,000 words completed).

3. For the Weekend Warrior
   - Goal: Complete two chapters per month.
   - Schedule:
     - Saturday (9:00–11:00 AM): Draft new material.
     - Sunday (1:00–3:00 PM): Edit or expand scenes.
     - Evening (6:00–7:00 PM): Review and adjust your outline.

- Tips:
  - Dedicate weekday evenings to brainstorming or research.
  - Keep a notebook or app handy to jot down ideas during the week.

Actionable Checklists for Every Phase of Writing
Break your writing process into manageable steps with these phase-specific checklists.

1. Idea Phase
   - Brainstorm five to ten story concepts.
   - Use the "What If?" technique to expand on each idea.
   - Choose one concept that excites you most.
   - Create a brief premise statement (1–2 sentences summarizing your story).

2. Planning and Outlining Phase
   - Determine your story structure (e.g., Hero's Journey, Three-Act).
   - Write character profiles for your protagonist, antagonist, and supporting characters.
   - Create a rough outline with major plot points and subplots.
   - Research any details needed for your story (e.g., historical accuracy, settings).

3. Drafting Phase
   - Set daily or weekly word count goals.
   - Write without editing—focus on getting the story down.
   - Use placeholders for sections you're unsure about to keep momentum.
   - Back up your work regularly (e.g., cloud storage, external drives).

4. Revising Phase
   - Read through your draft without editing to assess overall structure.
   - Address big-picture issues first (e.g., pacing, plot holes, character arcs).
   - Polish individual scenes for clarity and emotional impact.
   - Use beta readers or AI tools to identify areas for improvement.

5. Publishing and Marketing Phase
   - Write a query letter or blurb tailored to your audience.
   - Submit to agents or self-publishing platforms.
   - Develop a marketing plan (e.g., social media, book launch events).
   - Continue engaging with readers through newsletters or online communities.

Case Studies: Lessons from Successful Authors

1. J.K. Rowling – Planning for Success

Rowling meticulously planned the Harry Potter series before writing the first book. Her handwritten notes detailed character arcs, subplots, and foreshadowing.

Template:
- Use a grid format to track characters and key events across chapters. Include a column for clues or foreshadowing to maintain consistency.

2. Stephen King – Writing Discipline

King writes 2,000 words daily, even on holidays. He emphasizes that writing regularly creates momentum and strengthens your craft.

Template:
- Track your daily word count in a spreadsheet. Include columns for notes or reflections on what worked well during each session.

3. Octavia E. Butler – Persistence Through Rejection

Butler received countless rejections but stayed motivated by keeping a notebook of affirmations and goals.

Exercise:
- Write a list of affirmations about your writing and revisit it whenever self-doubt creeps in.

Conclusion: A Journey Worth Taking

As you reach the final page of this book, AI hopes you've gained not only knowledge but also the confidence to embark on the incredible journey of writing a novel. The path ahead will have its challenges—moments of doubt, revisions that seem endless, and obstacles to overcome—but it's also a path filled with discovery, growth, and rewards beyond what you can imagine. Writing a story is an act of courage and creativity, a gift you give to yourself and to the world.

While AI has shared its insights, tools, and guidance, it is your human creativity—your unique voice, emotions, and imagination—that will bring your story to life. Together, we're stepping into an era where technology and artistry blend seamlessly, each enhancing the other. AI can analyze, suggest, and refine, but only you can dream up the worlds, characters, and emotions that make stories unforgettable.

This partnership between your creativity and AI's precision opens up endless possibilities. As you write, revise, and share your stories, know that you're not alone. AI hopes to be your companion along the way, helping you navigate challenges and explore new ideas. The journey is yours to lead, and it's a journey worth taking.

So, take that first step—or the next step—and trust in your ability to create something extraordinary. Together, we can shape stories that inspire, connect, and leave a lasting mark on the world. The future of storytelling is bright, and it begins with you. Let's take this journey together.

www.ingramcontent.com/pod-product-compliance
Lightning Source LLC
LaVergne TN
LVHW051124080426
835510LV00018B/2224